BOCA RATON
A PICTORIAL HISTORY

by Donald W. Curl and John P. Johnson

The News has kept pace with hometown expansion

Have you seen the latest *News?*

Once upon a time, the latest news in Boca Raton arrived as an amateur collection of local tidbits earnestly assembled by a local physician and churned out by mimeograph. The publication was distributed as often as time permitted, and was called *The Pelican.*

Today, *The News* has a flamingo for its standard bearer, and is a daily publication under the wing of a major public corporation, Knight Ridder Inc., headquartered in Miami and parent of twenty-nine daily newspapers in the United States. Now in its thirty-sixth year, *The News* is larger, more sophisticated and high-tech than ever—yet it remains as solidly hometown as that day in 1955, when a local banker convinced the Chamber of Commerce this coastal hamlet of 4,000 residents needed its own newspaper.

The *Boca Raton News* was born, thanks to that banker, Tom Fleming, and the first publishers, Lora and Robert Britt. When the first regular weekly edition appeared on the streets December 2, 1955, the editor was Margaret Olsson and the news was all about local business and civic groups. In 1959, Halford Houser became the editor, with Clay Riley as advertising manager. Still a small operation, *The News* had grown to twice a week. By 1963, pioneer Arizona journalist Oliver Jaynes had acquired 83 percent of *The News* stock, while Tom Fleming retained 17 percent.

Along the way, a group of management employees at the *Miami Herald* offered to buy the *Boca Raton News,* and eventually the acquisition occurred. In 1969, *The News* was a wholly-owned subsidiary of Knight Newspapers, which merged with Ridder Publications Inc. in 1974. *The News* had further expanded, gradually becoming a six-day afternoon publication. Over the same period of time, Boca Raton had blossomed into a young city of 10,000 or 12,000 with a new state university and the burgeoning presence of major corporate citizens.

On March 17, 1978, the *Boca Raton News* made history and garnered a mention in the *Miami Herald,* which reported the unprecedented "Extra" edition published that morning in Boca Raton. The newspaper's one and only "Extra" was prompted by the occurrence of a true hometown tragedy—the loss of two Boca Raton teenagers, Cindy Rediger and John Futch.

In 1980, Clement C. Winke, Jr., became publisher of *The News.* During the decade of the 1980s, few metropolitan areas experienced the fast-track pace of growth witnessed throughout South Palm Beach County. Paralleling the area's directional mandate, *The News* expanded its coverage of Delray Beach with a new newspaper to serve that city in 1983. Subsequently, three major events have punctuated the proud history of *The News'* hometown journalism: conversion to a seven-day morning edition in June 1986; the addition of a weekly edition for Boynton Beach in 1988; the recent expansion of that edition to seven days, along with publishing a weekly newspaper in Deerfield Beach, in September 1990.

On October 11, 1990, concurrent with this latest expansion, *The News* launched an entirely transformed publication as innovative as any newspaper in the United States, and destined to be studied and admired by forward-thinking publishers everywhere. *The News* of the 1990s—about Boca Raton, Delray Beach, Boynton Beach and Deerfield Beach—proves that hometown journalism was a good idea all along.

THE NEWS

BOCA RATON ◆ DELRAY BEACH ◆ BOYNTON BEACH ◆ DEERFIELD BEACH

Boca Raton got its first Bank in 1956 when the First Bank and Trust Company of Boca Raton was formed by local businessmen. It, along with the Boca Raton National Bank, served the growing community for many years.

In the early 1980s the burgeoning Boca Raton market attracted many of the large state-wide banking institutions as well as some from out of state, and by the end of 1982, no bank existed that was headquartered in the city.

In 1983, a group of local bankers, many of whom had previously been associated with the above named institutions, backed by local investors, organized Boca Bank, "For Boca People . . . By Boca People." On October 23, Boca's new "home town" bank opened its doors in the old Boca Mall on Federal Highway. The bank grew rapidly, establishing additional offices in Town Center, on South Federal Highway, and in 1986 in the new Boca Bank Corporate Centre in west Boca. In late 1990, the bank will open an office in the new Mizner Park complex being developed downtown on the site of the old Boca Mall, thus coming full circle back to its original site.

The directors, officers and staff of Boca Bank take pride in having participated in the publication of this historical look at our city and area.

Boca Bank

The authors wish to dedicate this book to Peggy McCall.
The source of all Boca Raton history.

Richard A. Horwege, Editor
Barbara A. Bolton, Project Manager

Library of Congress Cataloging in Publication Data:

Curl, Donald Walter, 1935-
        Boca Raton: a pictorial history / by Donald W. Curl and John P. Johnson.
            p.   cm.
        Includes bibliographical references.
        Includes index.
        ISBN 0-89865-792-X
        1. Boca Raton (Fla.)—History—Pictorial works. 2. Boca Raton
        (Fla.)—Description—Views.   I. Johnson, John p., 1946- . II. Title.
        F319.b6C85   1990
        975.9'32—dc20   90-47870
                                CIP

Printed in the United States of America

C O N T E N T S

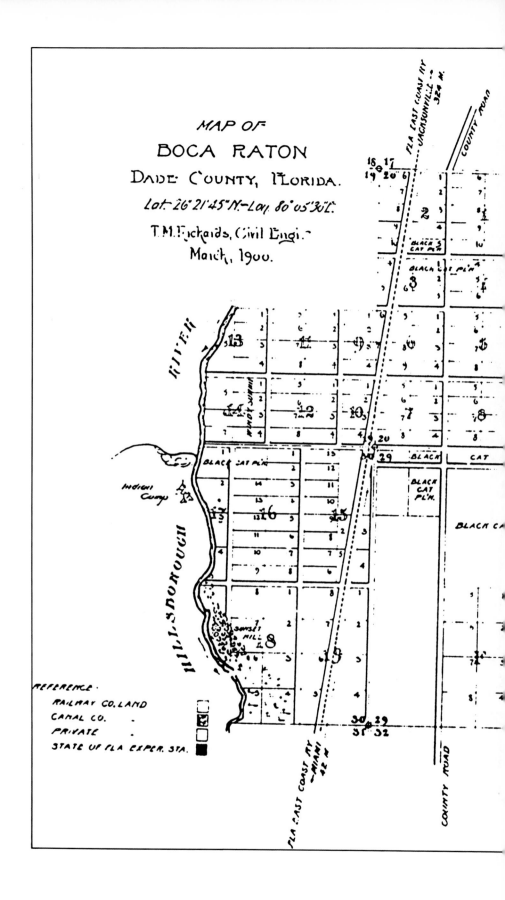

ACKNOWLEDGEMENTS

In the spring of 1988, Ray Fox of the Boca Bank and Clem Winke, publisher of the *Boca Raton News*, joined in a cooperative effort to publish this pictorial history of Boca Raton. The authors thank both Mr. Fox and Mr. Winke for selecting them for the job. We also apologize for the time it has taken to complete the work. Obviously many individuals made contributions towards the research and writing of this book. Nan Dennison of the Historical Society of Palm Beach County gave her usual cheerful help to the project. Members, officers, and trustees of the Boca Raton Historical Society also contributed knowledge, clippings, photographs, corrections, criticisms, and sometimes even sympathy. Eunice Canty, Marylew Redd, Anne Merrill, Kathy Dickenson, and Myrtle Fleming all deserve special mention as do Paula Long, the society's administrator, and, most deserving of all, the society's volunteer archivist, Peggy McCall. Peggy was always available to answer questions, find material, make telephone calls, and identify faded faces on old photographs. Particular thanks go to Fred Eckel, Karen Milano, Gloria Thompson, William Watkins, Carl Lawrence, and Mrs. Arthur A. Johnson. Finally, the authors acknowledge the generosity of the Boca Raton Historical Society in allowing us to use its large photographic collection. All photographs in this book, unless specifically labeled otherwise, are from the Boca Raton Historical Society collection.

Boca Raton's first settler was Capt. Thomas Moore Rickards, a land surveyor for several of Florida's early railroads. Photographed here with his survey crew at a temporary camp site somewhere along the Withlacoochee River about 1880, Rickards, center, traveled by wagon, boat, and railroad throughout Florida and in the 1880s purchased fifty acres on the Florida Coast Line Canal just north of Lake Boca Raton.

C H A P T E R   I

THE PIONEER ERA

The first thing taught a newcomer is to pronounce the name *Boca Ra-tone.* As Boca Raton grew in size and prestige, residents have taken particular pride in the name. Very few communities along the southeastern Florida coast can claim a name of Spanish origin. Amongst the Delrays, Deerfields, Boyntons, and Lauderdales, Boca Raton stands out, the very sound conjuring up images of conquestadores, Indian princesses, and even pirates.

Boca means mouth, and in Spanish as well as English, often describes the mouth of a river or an ocean inlet. Unfortunately, the most obvious literal translation of *Boca Raton* is then "rat's mouth." Many local citizens, refusing to live in Rat's Mouth, have attempted to find an archaic nautical term for the name's derivation. For years the Chamber of Commerce translated the names as "harbor of hidden rocks," while another source essayed "hidden rocks that gnaws and frets a ship's cable." Daniel Austin, a professor of biological science at Florida Atlantic University, and David McJunkin, a former geography graduate student, in a *Spanish River Papers* article say they can find "no etymological source . . . to support these interpretations." Moreover, they point out that *rata* is the Spanish word for rat, while *raton* means mouse. Does this mean Boca Raton should be translated "mouse's mouth?" Austin and McJunkin say probably no, and suggest alternatives.

The two scholars studied dozens of maps dating from the sixteenth century to the twentieth. On the very first map they discovered a Ratone River flowing into upper Biscayne Bay. Across the bay the inlet was labeled Boca Ratones. The name then is first associated with northern Biscayne Bay and not the current Palm Beach County city. On each succeeding map until the early nineteenth century, they continued to find this Boca Raton. On an 1823 map its location shifts to the new site in today's Palm Beach County. The name is given to both the lake and the inlet, which according to an early source, "is very seldom open." Earlier maps hinted at the inlet's condition, calling it *Rio Seco*, or "dry river."

One of the earliest legends of Boca Raton tells of pirate gold, buried either on the ocean beach or on the shores of Lake Boca Raton. Often either Captain Kidd or "Blackbeard" are said to have used the lake as a refuge between their plundering expeditions on the Spanish Main. One Boca Raton pioneer recalled the story of pirates who buried fourteen kegs of gold before Indians massacred all but two. The surviving pirates made their way to Pensacola, where one, near death, gave his rescuers a map showing the buried gold. The bearings on the map consisted of a tree and an iron peg. A fisherman living near the inlet found the iron peg and asked the map owners for half the treasure in return for showing them the location. When they refused, he removed the peg and threw it into the ocean, making sure no one would ever find the gold. Actually, since the Palm Beach County inlet was rarely open, few eighteenth-century

Henry Morrison Flagler's Florida East Coast Railway proceeded south from West Palm Beach in 1895 with stations at Lake Worth, Lantana, Hypoluxo, Boynton Beach, Linton (Delray), and Boca Raton. Captain Rickards returned to Lake Boca Raton and surveyed several hundred acres for the railroad. Most of the land was divided into ten-acre tracts and offered for sale as homesteads for agriculture and orange groves. In addition to acting as superintendent of the fifty-acre orange grove owned by the railroad, Rickards cared for his own grove which he named Black Cat Plantation.

buccaneers could have sought refuge on the calm waters of the inland lake. The legends of Boca Raton obviously refer to the older Biscayne Bay location.

Austin and McJunkin also answer the translation question. They mention that one early meaning of *raton* is dragging or hauling. Thus the name could refer to a shallow inlet accessible only to small boats which could be dragged or hauled across shallow water. Some evidence for this meaning can be found in the current Haulover Beach of upper Biscayne Bay. Nonetheless, they believe another possible translation is really the key to the name Boca Raton. In Spanish literature of the sixteenth and seventeenth centuries *raton* could refer to a cowardly thief. This makes possible the translation "thieves' inlet." As evidence they point to a report of Brother Villareal, left by Pedro Menendez, the Spanish governor of Florida, to establish a mission to the Tequesta Indians on Biscayne Bay in the mid-sixteenth century. Brother Villareal complained that the Indians were thieves. Almost two centuries later, Spanish priests still accused the same Indians of stealing. Accordingly, the inlet acquired the name from its location near the village of thieving Indians.

Although Charles Pierce in *Pioneer Life in Southeast Florida* mentions Boca Raton as a resting place for the barefoot mailmen making their trips down the beach from Lake Worth to Biscayne Bay in the 1880s, only in the 1890s is the name applied to an actual settlement. Around 1895, Capt. Thomas Moore Rickards settled on the north shore of Lake Boca Raton where he built a

house from timbers salvaged from the ocean beach. This house, the first in Boca Raton, stood on the east side of the Florida Coast Line Canal, near the present-day Palmetto Park Road. Rickards, Ohio born and Missouri bred, first came to Florida in 1876 to escape northern winters. A trained civil engineer and well educated for his time, he wrote letters to his hometown newspaper on his trip from Missouri telling of the economic conditions and travel hardships he found along the way.

In Alachua County the thriving farms convinced Rickards to settle and he took up a homestead at Candler on Lake Weir, about thirteen miles from Gainesville. Three years later a visiting nephew told of his three hundred orange trees ready to bear, fifty lemon trees already producing fruit, and "bananas by the hundreds." He also used his engineering skills and surveyed the Withlacoochee River for the state of Florida. The state asked him to determine if the river was navigable and the cost to open it for steamboat traffic.

During this period Rickards also began to buy land in South Florida. By 1892 he owned tracts on the New and Hillsborough rivers and fifty acres on Lake Boca Raton. In that year he made a trip with his son Jim and a friend from Missouri to investigate his land holdings. Rickards and his party came by steamer down the Indian River to Jupiter, then took the short-lived "Celestial Railroad" to Juno on Lake Worth, continued down the lake to Palm Beach, and then hitched a ride

Captain Rickards built Boca Raton's first house in the mid-1890s for his wife, three daughters, and two sons. The two-story wood frame building with porches was a typical architectural style of the pioneer period. It overlooked the Florida Coast Line Canal on the east side, just south of the present-day Palmetto Park Bridge. When Rickards built Boca Raton's second house, this became the home of George A. Long and it was razed in 1904. The Kathleen, a steam-powered passenger, freight, and mail boat, had a twice-weekly route between Palm Beach and Miami. A toll chain extended across the canal at the Rickards's house and his sons collected tolls from passing boats.

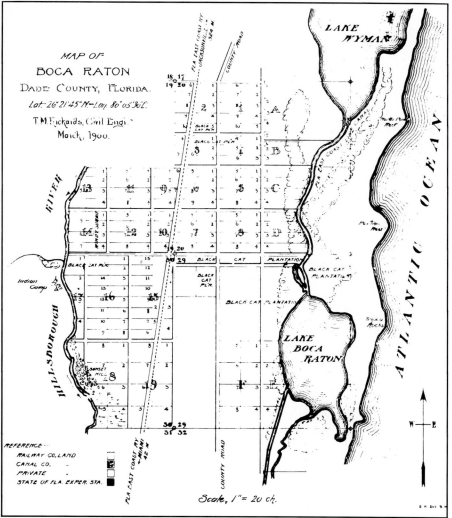

In 1896 Captain Rickards completed the first survey of Boca Raton. This surveyed area was part of Dade County until Palm Beach County was created in 1909. The survey was recorded in March 1890 and featured Rickards's Black Cat Plantation near the Florida East Coast Railway line. The Florida Coast Line Canal, that was first dredged in 1882 between Lake Wyman and Lake Boca Raton, was later enlarged and named the Intracoastal Waterway. The Hillsborough River, known today as the El Rio Canal, divided the small settlement from a Seminole Indian camp west of the river.

Capt. Thomas Moore Rickards (1845-1928), a native of Ohio, was a civil engineer for the Florida East Coast Railway and made regular reports to James E. Ingraham, FEC vice president and land commissioner. The Model Land Company, formed to sell the thousands of acres granted the railroad by Florida, circulated pamphlets and brochures designed to encourage settlement by advertising the opportunities of oranges and pineapple production. For the first decade of Boca Raton's development, Rickards managed the railroad's interests in the little settlement.

on the schooner *Emily B* to the Fort Lauderdale House of Refuge which they used as a base for their explorations.

To explore the area Rickards brought a folding canvas boat that extended to twelve feet and could carry five hundred pounds. He found his various tracts of South Florida land, and after a visit to Lemon City and Cocoanut Grove on Biscanye Bay, he returned to Candler, though determined now to move to his Boca Raton land. As several devastating freezes had destroyed his citrus groves, he hoped to make a new start in the tropical wilderness. Probably the 1894-1895 freeze, the same one that decided Henry M. Flagler to extend his Florida East Coast Railway (FEC) from West Palm Beach to Miami, also convinced Rickards to move to Boca Raton. He brought his family to the wilderness farm, which he named Black Cat Plantation, before Flagler's railroad arrived in 1895.

With the coming of the FEC, Rickards's talents as a civil engineer were once more called upon and he became the railroad's local agent. When Flagler also made him the agent for the Model Land Company, he platted the first settlement. Rickards planted orange groves for both Flagler and James E. Ingraham, the railroad's vice president, and cleared and planted fifty acres of his own land. His success allowed him in the late 1890s to build a large new house just east of the railroad tracks and south of Palmetto Park Road. Jacqueline Ashton, in *Boca Raton: From Pioneer Days to the Fabulous Twenties* says that the nine-room frame house "was the most imposing in the settlement." Almost all accounts note his large library.

The February 1900 issue of *The Homeseeker*, the publication of the Model Land Company used to promote land sales in Southeast Florida, told of the booming orange and pineapple industry in Boca Raton. The article said that while the town had few citizens, Rickards, acting as agent for any number of landowners, had cleared and planted orange groves and pineapple fields and that other settlers had produced crops of tomatoes, eggplants, beans, and potatoes.

In 1902 George Ashley Long, another civil engineer and friend of Rickards, moved his family to Boca Raton. Long, a Bostonian and a Harvard graduate, came to Florida seeking a cure for ill-health. He first settled at Interlachen where he both regained his health and

*Mrs. T. M. "Lizzy" Rickards, wife of
Captain Rickards and mother of their five
children, settled here in the mid-1890s.
The small community boasted orange
groves, pineapple fields, and vegetable
farms but also subsisted on native plants,
animals, and fish. After devastating
hurricanes, crop failures, and hard freezes,
not to mention a variety of local pests, the
Rickards family gave up on Florida and
moved to North Carolina in 1906.*

established himself as an engineer and a citrus grower.
When the freeze of 1894-95 destroyed his groves he
decided to join his friend Rickards in Boca Raton. With
his wife Catherine and three children, Long moved into
the first Rickards house on the canal.

In this period James E. Ingraham recruited a colony
of Japanese farmers to settle a colony in northern Boca
Raton and commissioned Rickards to see that it was
established. The founder of the colony, Jo Sakai,
received a degree from the New York University School
of Finance and came armed with a letter of
introduction from its dean. Sakai thought of the Boca
Raton colony as only one of a group spread across the
state of Florida. As a promoter, he saw these colonies
as a refuge for the ever growing population of Japan
and as profit-making investments.

Lending an air of mystery to the project, Count
Masakuni Okudaira, rumored to be a member of the
Japanese royal household, assisted Sakai in his efforts
to secure exit permits and passports for his settlers.
The government discouraged the emigration of young
men at this time because of the Russo-Japanese War.
Floridians, always anxious for more settlers, received

Sakai's proposal for settlements with enthusiasm. The
Florida East Coast Railway and other private investors
promised him land and Governor William Jennings gave
his official endorsement.

On Christmas Day 1903, Sakai arrived in Boca Raton
to examine a proposed location for a colony. Much of
this tract belonged to the Model Land Company.
Rickards met with Sakai and showed him the tract.
Rickards must have been a good salesman, for Sakai
departed two days later sold on the Boca Raton location.

The first colonists arrived late the following year.
They named their settlement Yamato, or "large
peaceful country," an ancient name for Japan. Contrary
to local legend the name had no connection with the
way the Japanese pronounced tomato. The earliest
arrivals immediately began clearing land for planting.
Sakai originally proposed that his colonies should grow
silk, rice, tea, tobacco, and pineapples. Climatic
conditions and the high prices to be gained from
pineapples, quickly dictated a one crop production for
Yamato.

The virgin hammock land was both difficult to clear
and to cultivate. This limited production as one man

Seminole Indians traded feathers, furs, and food stuffs with the pioneers at frontier outposts like this one at Rickards's homestead on the canal. The Seminoles used cypress dugout canoes for travel throughout southern Florida. The pioneers lived mostly on available foods at hand. The bud of the native palmetto was made into salads and cooked in milk like asparagus. From the pioneer farms came tomatoes, peppers, beans, squash, and cucumbers. Winter squash, pumpkins, lettuce, corn, potatoes, and watermelons were grown in the home gardens. Native guava were made into jelly, cooked and canned like peaches, or made into pies. Cocoplums and sea grapes made a good jelly. The mastic, a small yellow plum-like fruit, mulberries and huckelberries, pond apples, and several varieties of bananas were available to the pioneer diet.

Contact between the Seminoles and the pioneers benefited both cultures as each group had items of value for sale and for trade. These Seminole boys are waiting for the train on the freight platform of the Boca Raton railroad station.

Beginning in 1883, floating steam-powered dredges connected the existing rivers and lakes along the east coast of Florida to create an inland navigation canal. This view is looking south on the Florida Coast Line Canal with Captain Rickards's house on the left.

could care for a field of only about an acre. Pineapples planted in cleared bare ground soon had their hearts filled with wind blown sand, choking off life. Although a ground cover of mulch solved this problem, the mulch meant hand weeding of the fields. One contemporary description tells of the rigors this caused for the farmers. The sharp curved spines of the plant demanded that they wear heavy gloves to protect their hands and two shirts and two pairs of pants to protect the rest of their body from the thorns. The swarms of flies and mosquitos also forced the wearing of headnets. As pineapple cultivation took place in the summer, this costume made the job almost unbearable.

Although the work proved far more demanding than the Japanese had imagined, the continued high prices for pineapples, the settlers' dedication to hard labor ("there is not a lazy bone in the body of these people"), and the slow, but steady stream of new immigrants, all began to produce results. By November 1906 one writer called their success in the tropical wilderness "almost phenomenal." At that time they had fifty acres planted in pineapples with other acreage devoted to citrus fruit and vegetables. The settlers had also completed eight houses and several sheds.

On a trip to Jacksonville to request the United States government establish a post office at Yamato, Sakai told a reporter that he had assured rapid growth for the colony by hiring an agent in Japan who sent to Florida the "pick of the Japanese agriculturists." He also said the colony was intensely patriotic working to advance the general welfare of the state which all the Japanese "have adopted for their future home." This permanent connection was shown when Sakai brought his wife Sada to Yamato in 1906 and began to raise a family, and when the other men sent to Japan for their wives and

families or for brides. As the families grew, the original primitive housing became inadequate and new and bigger houses were built.

The settlement continued to grow and prosper. By 1908 its population had reached forty people who cultivated seventy acres of pineapples and one hundred acres of citrus and vegetables. Moreover, interest in Yamato continued high in Japan. Several prominent Japanese men visited the settlement that year, and a four-part illustrated article on the colony written by Sakai appeared in a Japanese newspaper.

Nonetheless, 1908 marked the high point for Yamato. Late in the year a blight struck the colony's pineapple fields, wiping out much of its most important cash crop. By the time production could be restored, competition from Cuba had destroyed the domestic pineapple market. Moreover, a wave of anti-Japanese sentiment in California spilled over into Florida. Thus 1912-1913 saw attempts on both state and national levels to prevent the Japanese from owning land. The hard-working qualities of the Japanese of Yamato and their desire to adapt to American "ideas in manner of living and dress" had made them many friends. Consequently, Florida never passed any discriminatory legislation. Still, the discussion of such laws and the anti-Japanese sentiments expressed by some, virtually ended their migration into the state.

After Sakai died in North Carolina in 1923, Sada and their five daughters returned to Japan. While other colonists also went back to Japan, a few families remained. Some still lived at Yamato when the 1941 attack on Pearl Harbor produced a new wave of anti-Japanese sentiment. In May 1942 they received notice to vacate all land west of the railroad so that the site could become an Army Air Corps base.

An FEC railroad crew poses just south
of the station in Boca Raton. In 1900
The Homeseeker, *a Flagler publication
designed to promote interest in
Southeast Florida and encourage use of
the railroad, reported on extensive
clearing and development of acreage in
Boca Raton. In the distance is the
settlement's first railroad station,
similar in size and architectural design
to the stations in Delray and Deerfield.
To the right is the FEC Commissary
with express agency and post office
operated by Captain Rickards's sons,
Thomas M., Jr., and James C. Rickards.*

*George Ashley Long (1854-1929) from
Massachusetts, settled in Boca Raton in
1902. Long, a Harvard educated civil
engineer and Florida citrus grower was a
friend of Captain Rickards and a welcome
addition to the settlement. Long was
joined by his wife Catherine (Katie), and
three children, George J., Helen Mary, and
Hatty. Later, in 1909, F. Vinton Long was
the first white male child born in Boca
Raton. Long's farm, the Old Colony
Plantation, had it's own electricity,
running water, and an irrigation system.
After Captain Rickards left Boca Raton,
George Long became the local agent for
the FEC and its Model Land Company.*

Boca Raton's second house was built in 1902 by Captain Rickards on present-day Royal Palm Road. When the Rickards family left the town, George Long's family lived here. The farm was irrigated by pumping water into the elevated tank and then gravity fed to the water pipes in the fields.

Looking north along Dixie Highway the original FEC packing house can be seen in the distance just east of the tracks. Later purchased by George Long, it was renamed Long's Packing House and used for all community purposes, such as elections, meetings of the Board of Trade, social events, and the first school.

Nonetheless, unlike the Japanese of California, no Yamato farmers found themselves settled in internment camps.

One of the last members of Yamato to survive, George Sukeji Morikami, built a fortune in land in the area west of Delray Beach through years of dedicated work. Granted American citizenship in 1967 at the age of eighty-two, Morikami decided to repay the debt he felt to his adopted country by donating land for the south county park that bears his name. Today, the memory of that small and completely lost colony of Japanese-Americans is remembered through Morikami's park and the small gem-like Japanese Museum that forms its centerpiece.

In 1903 a hurricane struck the southeastern Florida coast. Once more a natural disaster wiped out all that Thomas Rickards had worked for, flooding his fields and destroying his groves. Discouraged with Florida, and with an ill wife, the Rickards began spending the summers in the North Carolina mountains. In 1906

they decided to move there permanently. Although George Long's farm had also suffered a great deal of damage in the 1903 hurricane, he refused to give up. When Rickards left, Long now assumed his many duties with the railroad and land company and even became postmaster. He also bought the Rickards's house and installed a power plant, and built a packing house which according to Ashton, became the unofficial community center.

Moreover, the settlement was growing. Frank H. Chesebro and his wife Jeanette settled on sixty acres purchased from the Model Land Company in 1903. Bert and Annie Raulerson arrived that same year. In 1906 Annie's brother, Perry Purdom, brought his wife, Florence, and their six children to Boca Raton. The Chesebros, from Michigan, joined the majority of the little town's northern population. The Raulersons and Purdoms took pride in their "Florida Cracker" origins.

With the six Purdom children now in town, and two of the young sisters forced to walk to Deerfield School,

This rare interior photograph was possibly taken at George Long's second packing house about 1908. These seasonal workers are packing oranges for shipment by the railroad to northern markets. This simple wood frame building was located on the railroad siding south of Palmetto Park Road and east of the tracks.

Boca Raton citizens decided to petition the school board to establish a school in the community. At the time, Boca Raton was in Dade County, although Palm Beach County would be created in 1909. The School Board agreed to furnish a teacher if the community could supply a building. George Long volunteered his packing house as a temporary school which opened in the fall 1908. Donated materials and labor allowed the construction of a permanent one-room school before the end of the year.

While Boca Raton schools have had many outstanding teachers, one of the earliest went on to become a leading American scientist. Laurence McKinley Gould served as teacher of the Boca Raton school from the fall of 1914 to the summer of 1916. Although only eighteen and himself a recent graduate of high school in Michigan, Gould quickly made his presence felt in the small community. A forceful and long remembered teacher, he also organized community gatherings, helped found a Sunday School class, and with his students, published Boca Raton's first newspaper.

From the beginning, Gould planned only a sojourn in Boca Raton. His ambition to return to Michigan and the university at Ann Arbor to study law was well known. He lived with the Chesebros, made friends with Bill and Peggy Young (a Scots couple and she served as postmistress), enjoyed the ocean, hunted in the Everglades, and saved his money for college. Gould enrolled at the University of Michigan in the fall of 1916, though the United States entered World War I before he received his degree. After serving in the ambulance corps in Italy, France, and Germany, Gould returned to the university where his interest in law was sidetracked by his love of rocks. He graduated with a degree in geology in 1921 and in 1925 received a Sc.D. in glacial geology. As a faculty member at the University of Michigan he participated in a number of scientific expeditions to places like Greenland and Baffin Island.

Gould's education and scientific experience prepared him for one of the most renowned expeditions of the century: Admiral Richard Byrd's first Antarctica expedition. When Byrd reached Antarctica on December 30, 1928, he chose a campsite which he named "Little America." Gould, who had been named second in command, was sent ashore to oversee the erection of the shelters and to make preparations for the winter.

After completing the camp, Gould with only two companions made a trip of exploration to the Rockefeller mountains in early March. A major storm hit their camp and wrecked their small plane. A *New York Times* headline of March 18 proclaimed, "Gould, two companions, are missing in Antarctic Wastes." After the storm passed, Byrd was able to rescue the stranded men, returning them to Little America on March 22. During the next Antarctica summer Gould made a 338-mile, four-month trip overland by dog sled collecting data and specimens.

Gould returned home with the Byrd Expedition in early 1930, resuming his post at the University of Michigan. His work in Antarctica was honored by a David Livingston Gold Metal in 1930 and a Congressional Gold Metal in 1931. In the same year a New York publisher brought out his account of the adventure in a book entitled *Cold.* In 1932 Gould

Joe Myrick makes wooden bean crates at Long's packing house in 1915.

became professor of geography and geology at Carlton College in Minnesota, and from 1945 to 1962 served as Carlton's president. He then became professor of geological science at the University of Arizona. In 1979 at age eighty-three he returned to Antarctica to commemorate the fiftieth anniversary of the historic expedition.

Gould was still a teacher at the Boca Raton school when Harley D. Gates and his new wife Harriette arrived in Boca Raton. Gates, a real estate salesman in Poultney, Vermont, suffered from asthma. When he visited Florida in 1913 seeking relief from this condition, he caught a fifty-pound red snapper off the shores of Boca Raton. Gates was so impressed with the area that before returning to Vermont he purchased five acres of land on the canal at Palmetto Park Road from George Long. Gates brought his bride to a West Indian style bungalow which he had constructed of cement blocks. Wide screen porches surrounded the house which had running water, considered a great luxury at the time, and a telephone. Harley Gates called his property Palmetto Park Plantation, and it gave its name to Boca Raton's principal east-west road.

From the first, Gates worked to encourage settlers to come to Boca Raton, extolling the virtues of the small community to friends and business associates across the country, and particularly mentioning the land bargains available. Since Boca Raton had no hotels, prospective real estate clients were often invited to stay with the Gates family. When this became too great a burden for Harriette, now a young mother, Harley Gates built four small guest cottages on Palmetto Park Road, naming them for states. One prime real estate transaction Gates made was the sale of his own bungalow in 1923 at the beginning of the land boom to Stanley Harris of Vancouver. The house had cost Gates $3,500 to build in 1915. He sold it for $10,000. Harris added a tower and garages, stuccoed the cement blocks, painted it pink, and renamed the now Mediterranean-style house Casa Rosa.

Real estate developments such as those promoted by Gates, the hard surfacing of the Dixie Highway, and the extension of the Ocean Boulevard to the south county line, all helped prepare Boca Raton for the land boom of the 1920s. Nonetheless, as the twenties began, the town remained a small, friendly community of farmers, growing citrus and vegetables for the winter market.

At the turn of the century most of the pine scrub woodland had to be cleared by hand before being cultivated as farmland. Captain Rickards supervised the operations to create the Chesebro plantation.

Frank Howard Chesebro, an early pioneer from Michigan, purchased sixty acres from Captain Rickards in 1902. He built this house and barn in 1903 in the center of his pineapple plantation, south of present-day Camino Real, just east of the railroad tracks. With the help of his wife Jeanette (Nettie), son Harry, and daughters Esther and Ruth, the little farm prospered. In addition to the cash crop of pineapples, they also grew, packed, and shipped tomatoes, beans, peas, beets, turnips, onions, parsnips, and lettuce.

Frank H. Chesebro (1850-1936) pictured with his wife Nettie, was a community leader with a large pineapple plantation, vegetable farm, and packing house. His detailed diaries are an invaluable eye-witness account of life in the pioneer period. He was instrumental in building the town's first public school in 1908 and establishing the Boca Raton Board of Trade in 1915, but he vigorously opposed the incorporation of the town in 1925.

The Chesebro house was typical of wood frame architecture of the pioneer period. Train carloads of building material arrived at the station with lumber, shingles, lath, brick, and lime, as well as windows, doors, and hardware. Good carpenters could earn from $1.50 to $2.25 per day. A two-room cottage, without lath and plaster, but with a small front porch, cost about $140. Although most houses were set on brick piers, it was common to use terra-cotta flues instead of bricks for chimneys. The flues sold for about fifty cents per foot. A small four-room cottage cost around $275 and a neat six-room, lathed, plastered, and painted cottage could be built for about $750 worth of building materials.

Through the years as the farm thrived, the Chesebro house saw numerous additions. Barns and other outbuildings were constructed throughout the citrus groves and pineapples fields. Pineapples were the chief crop until a blight hit the fields and competition from Cuba ruined the industry in Florida. Then Chesebro turned exclusively to raising vegetables for local and northern markets.

Plowing and cultivating large agricultural fields was hard work, whether by hand, mule-drawn equipment, or this large steam-powered tractor.

Small barns and outbuildings were often thatch-covered, like this cypress-framed shack used for animals, and to store equipment, seed, and baskets. These field hands worked at the Chesebro plantation.

At the Chesebro farm, vegetables like tomatoes, beans, eggplants, and peppers were picked by field hands and taken by horse and wagon to the packing house.

This obviously posed photograph shows Homer Goddard, Sr., a man named Lee, and Will Demery, three nursery workers on a watermelon break at the Chesebro nursery.

The pioneer farmers copied the architectural style of the thatched-roof dwellings of the Seminoles for temporary outbuildings. Harry Chesebro, second son of Frank, is pictured here on the family farm.

A staged photograph of workers at the Chesebro Packing House that was built in 1907 for processing pineapples, oranges, and tomatoes. The large two-story building was located just east of the railroad tracks on the Chesebro farm.

IRISH POTATOES GROWN AT BOCA

A local farmer proudly displays his crop of Irish potatoes, an important segment of the area's vegetable farming business.

The local guide Joe Butler knew the best fishing spots in the river, along the canal, or in the lakes. Fish of all kinds, clams, oysters, shrimp, and turtles were plentiful along the beach and in the lakes. Wild game included ducks, quail, turkey, rabbits, and deer. Special treats included turtle eggs, bear steaks, and alligator tails.

The town's first wood-plank bridge was built in 1905 across the Hillsborough River to develop farmlands west of town. In 1905 there were only six resident families in Boca Raton and only twelve by 1923.

Laurence Gould (1896-) came from Michigan to teach public school in Boca Raton from 1914 to 1916. After World War I he attended the University of Michigan to earn three degrees in geology and in 1928 accompanied Admiral Richard Byrd on his famous expedition to Antarctica. He established the Geology Department in 1932 at Carlton College in Northfield, Minnesota, and was president of the college from 1945 to 1962. From 1962 until 1978 he was a professor at the University of Arizona.

Frank Chesebro's farm wagon doubled as Boca Raton's first school bus. From the fall of 1914 until the summer of 1916 Laurence Gould delivered children from the local farms to the town's only public school. Gould came to Boca Raton at the invitation of Frank Chesebro and lived at the Chesebro house. The school also doubled as a community church.

Boca Raton's formal school began in 1908 in a one-room schoolhouse on Northwest Second Avenue, north of Palmetto Park Road. Laurence Gould, the eighteen-year-old teacher, is pictured with his 1915 class for grades one through eight. Only white children attended public school in Boca Raton

until 1923 when Alex Hughes, a co-founder of Pearl City, organized the opening of Roadman Elementary for the children of the town's black community.

28

Laurence Gould also used Frank Chesebro's Model T Ford, Boca Raton's first automobile, to transport students to and from school.

Mrs. Hildreth Grey, a Yamato colony school teacher, with her 1918 class in front of a large steam tractor at the Yamato General Store. The store, located on Dixie Highway about a half a mile north of present-day Yamato Road, stocked clothing, shoes, pots and pans, watches, candy, tobacco, and all kinds of groceries.

Laurence Gould with good friend Susumu "Oscar" Kobayashi, a resident of the Yamato colony. Yamato, an ancient name for Japan, was the name adopted by Japanese farmers who settled in northwest Boca Raton in 1904. The colony specialized in raising pineapples until 1908 and then vegetables were shipped from the Yamato railroad station.

Mrs. Clementine Brown's class at Yamato school about 1919. Clementine was the wife of John Brown, who was later elected the town's first mayor. At this time the Smith, Richarson, and Montgomery families lived with several Japanese families at Yamato, a small farming community. Back row: Vernon Richardson, Walter Smith, Franklin Kamiya, Mrs. Brown, and Hazel Smith. Front row: Andy Montgomery, Yamauchi Kazu, Masuko Kamiya, and Kazuo Kamiya. The Yamato school closed in 1924.

The Boca Raton public school class poses about 1918. Front row (left to right) are Vinton Long, Pauline Raulerson, Clifford Purdon, Ivy Raulerson, and Vernon Richardson. Back row (left to right) are Grace Coombs, Myrtle Lee Raulerson, Iris Carroll, Bill Brenk, Evelyn Fisher, Ernestine Purdom, Arthur Brenk, and Johnnie Combs.

Perry Purdom and his wife Florence brought six children to the settlement in 1905. Purdom worked a vegetable farm on the dirt road leading west of town as a sharecropper. The children were Audrey, Viola, Eula, Thelma, Harry, and Jewell.

Bert and Annie Raulerson, with daughter Ivy, came to Boca Raton in 1903 and built this house about 1914 on West Palmetto Park Road. Their second daughter, Myrtle Lee was the first white female child born in Boca Raton. This two-story frame house, typical of the pioneer period, was relocated to Southwest Second Avenue and restored by Diane DeMarco in 1987.

William and Mamie Myrick, who moved from North Carolina, built this house in Boca Raton about 1914. Since no building permits were required at this time, it is still speculation whether this, or the Raulersons' is the oldest standing house in Boca Raton. George and Nellie Race purchased the Myrick house in 1917 and their only child Lillian Race Williams named it Singing Pines after the stand of Australian pine trees on the property. In 1975 the house was moved from 301 Southwest First Avenue by the Boca Raton Historical Society and the Junior Service League to Crawford Boulevard where it has become the Children's Museum.

This Myrick family portrait was taken on the front porch in 1916; left to right, Joe, Mamie, Bob, Aldah, and William. The Myrick house, later named Singing Pines, has always held local interest for its symmetrical entrance framed by a gable roof and six wooden Ionic columns.

Harley and Harriette Gates, who came from Vermont, built on the canal in 1914. This unusual West Indian bungalow was constructed of ornamental concrete block with a porch surrounding the entire house to capture the breezes. Gates specialized in raising fruit trees of every description at the estate they named Palmetto Park Plantation. Boca Raton's main east-west street was later named after the Gates' estate. In 1923 Gates sold the house to Stanley Harris who added a tower, garages, painted the house pink, and renamed it Casa Rosa. The house was a local landmark at the northwest end of the Palmetto Park Bridge until it was razed to build the Wildflower Restaurant.

Harley and Harriette Gates with their daughter, Imogene Alice, at their home. There was no local newspaper, so Harley and Hariette published articles in the Delray Beach News-Journal and the Miami Herald. Harley became a realtor and with Bert Raulerson and George Long formed the Boca Raton Land Company. Active in civic affairs, Gates served on the Town Council, was a municipal judge, a School Board trustee, and wrote numerous articles on early Boca Raton history.

Since the nearest tourist hotels were in Deerfield Beach or Delray, Harley Gates built several guest cottages in 1915 for prospective buyers of local real estate. Pictured here are George and Nellie Race who drove their automobile all the way from New York state. They rented the New York cottage on East Palmetto Park Road and in 1917 they moved with their daughter, Lillian, to the town permanently.

Built before World War I, Harley Gates's modest tourist cottage, Texas, displayed palm tree trunks for porch posts. Other houses were named for the states of Indiana and New York. In 1915 the town received a telephone line from Delray, established a Board of Trade, and built the Boca Raton Water and Light Company.

Bill Young and Bob Myrick showing off the latest hatchlings from the Myrick's little backyard alligator farm. Bill Young, a Scots sculptor and stone mason, came to Florida to work on the construction of Vizcaya, the Deering estate in Miami. He and his wife, Peg, moved to Boca Raton in 1915. After opening one of Boca Raton's first grocery stores in 1916, Peg became postmistress, relieving George Long of his nine-year service as postmaster.

John Brown came to Boca Raton with his mother, Nancy, and his brother, Charlie, in 1913. They purchased thirty acres and went into truck farming and road building. Brown's farm truck and steam roller were used to haul and crush rock for early town streets like Palmetto Park Road in 1913 and the widening of Dixie Highway in 1916. John Brown married Clementine Peterson in West Palm Beach in 1915 and they settled in Boca Raton.

Mr. and Mrs. Perley D. Kinney, with a local fishing guide, display a morning's catch at their boat dock just south of the Palmetto Park Bridge. Real estate developer Harley Gates and Kinney formed the Gates and Kinney subdivision north of Palmetto Park Road.

The first bridge across the Florida Coast Line Canal was built in 1917 on Palmetto Park Road. This manually operated drawbridge was tended by William and Eliza Townsend who lived in the adjoining house near the northeast corner. William Townsend was succeeded in 1919 by Lucas Douglas, resident bridgetender with his family until 1947. The 1928 concrete drawbridge at this location was replaced by the present drawbridge in 1987 and dedicated to Lucas Douglas.

A Sunday outing in 1916 of the Myrick family and friends at the Hillsboro Inlet Light Station. The lighthouse, constructed in 1907, became a popular local attraction for social and recreational events.

The Myrick party swimming in the Atlantic Ocean, near the Hillsboro Inlet. Although pioneer Floridians used the ocean for sailing, swimming, and social events, few of them built houses on the beach until the 1920s.

Boca Raton By The Sea was a popular recreation spot located on the north side of the inlet. This beach side club and marina was a local gathering place for dancing, boating, and fishing. Today this is the site of the Boca Beach Club.

The first bridge at the Boca Raton Inlet was a narrow fixed wooden span built in 1923 just west of the Boca Raton By The Sea. It was replaced in about 1930 as a part of Clarence Geist's project to dredge the inlet to allow members' yachts to dock at the Boca Raton Club. This manually-operated, one-lane drawbridge was replaced in 1963 when the present bridge was constructed and dedicated to Haven M. Ashe, a longtime bridgetender.

A 1923 view of the boat dock at Boca Raton By The Sea at the north side of the inlet looking toward the ocean. Fierce northeast winds and shifting sands often closed the inlet to navigation, making it an endless battle to keep the access open from the Atlantic Ocean into Lake Boca Raton.

Joseph A. "Tony" Brenk built this country grocery store with gasoline pumps on Northwest First Avenue and West Palmetto Park Road in 1918 and succeeded Peg Young as postmaster in 1919.

The first church in Pearl City, a small black community in Boca Raton, was the Macedonia African Methodist Episcopal (AME) Church of 1920. Built by farm workers, the now-stuccoed frame building still stands on Northeast Eleventh Street, on land donated by George Long.

George and Alberta Howard built this two-story house about 1920 on East Palmetto Park Road. At various times it was a doctor's office, a photography studio, and today houses the offices of McCall and Lynch Architects.

Boca Raton's second public elementary school was designed in the popular Mission style of architecture and built in 1924 by the Palm Beach County School Board. An auditorium was added in 1937 but the school was partially destroyed by fire in 1958. The third school in Boca Raton, J. C. Mitchell Elementary School, was built in 1958, although high school students traveled to Delray Beach until 1963 when Boca Raton High School opened.

Connecting the public rooms of the hotel with the guest rooms in the southern wing, the cloisters enclosed a great courtyard that was later landscaped with palms and other tropical plants, paved with exotic tiles, and finished with fountains and pools. The center portal provided an entrance to the hotel for those who arrived by yacht. The stubby Gothic columns are finished with capitals of crudely carved figures and animals. Here Mizner said he took his inspiration from a cloister at the University of Seville.

CHAPTER II

THE FABULOUS TWENTIES

The years following World War I saw the rapid development of the entire southeastern coast of Florida. National prosperity and the inexpensive automobile placed a winter vacation within the means of many members of the growing American middle class. Florida's balmy winter days acted as the magnet, drawing ever increasing numbers down the narrow Dixie Highway. Once the visitors heard the stories of the fortunes made by land investors and the promises of the state to levy no income or inheritance taxes, many decided to stay on and join this great adventure.

Real estate developers, Chamber of Commerce organizations, and local governments all launched campaigns to encourage more tourists and to sell land to those who came. Everyone heard the stories of cook, plumber, or housewife, who purchased a small inexpensive Miami lot in the late fall and by spring doubled or even quadrupled the original investment. It seemed that Florida could make anyone, willing to take the chance, rich.

Although a number of lots sold along Palmetto Park Road just before the war, in the first years of what became the great Florida land boom, Boca Raton remained a sleepy farming village. Still Harley Gates, its leading real estate agent, promoted his town. In a small pamphlet he told of the opportunities available for growing fruit and offered several hundred acres of prime Boca Raton land on good roads and close to the railroad for the cultivation of all kinds of citrus, pineapples, avocados, mangoes, guavas, coconuts, bananas, or papayas. While admitting that truck farming could lead to quicker returns, Gates called fruit "a more staple and surer proposition."

During the 1922-1923 season Gates, who realized that Miami had become the center of the South Florida real estate market, worked in the Magic City. There he met LaFayette Cooke of Cooke Springs, Alabama, who with his wife, Elizabeth, regularly spent part of each winter in the South Florida sunshine. Cooke, a businessman and banker, witnessed the beginnings of the land boom and by 1922 resolved to become part of the action. Gates brought the Alabaman up to Boca Raton and showed him the still untamed land south of Palmetto Park Road and east of the Dixie Highway that today contains much of downtown and the Royal Palm Yacht and Country Club. Before returning to Alabama in the spring, Cooke formed the South East Coast Land Company and purchased almost five hundred acres of Boca Raton property.

In September 1923 a short article in the *Palm Beach Post* gave details on Boca Raton's first boom-time development. Emphasizing its "high class" character, George A. Long announced plans for LaFayette Cooke's new

When Harley Gates built this small real estate office it gave no hint that Addison Mizner would soon attempt to turn Boca Raton into his vision of a Spanish city. The South Florida Sales Company, of which Gates was secretary-treasurer, developed the small four-block subdivisions of Kings Court and Kimberly Heights, and the two-block Elevado. All three were just north of Palmetto Park Road and close to downtown. South Florida Sales Company advertisements always mentioned its developments were close to Mizner's and that one could consequently expect quick profits from a purchase. The company also extended easy terms of 20 percent cash and 10 percent quarterly thereafter.

town site. These included laying rock on three miles of streets as well as furnishing curbs and sidewalks. These improvements, he said, would be made as lots in the subdivision sold. This development also brought to Boca Raton two new residents who over the coming years proved outstanding community leaders. Cooke asked his son-in-law and daughter, Jones Cleveland (J. C.) and Floy Mitchell, to come to Florida to oversee his investment.

The Mitchells arrived in Boca Raton on October 1, 1923, and immediately began efforts to sell the new subdivision. Harley Gates also continued to promote local real estate and George A. Long attempted to promote the little town. Long believed that incorporation was mandatory for the issuance of bonds for the needed improvements that would attract the attention of the developers. An October 1923 election gave voter approval to issue bonds for improvements and pay for the incorporation process. The Florida legislature then voted favorably in the spring of 1924 and Boca Raton became an incorporated town. Nonetheless, success eluded these efforts. Although bisected by the Dixie Highway and the tracks of the Florida East Coast Railway, Boca Raton's location almost forty-five miles north of Miami and twenty-four miles south of Palm Beach made it too isolated for most land speculators. The town continued to languish as up and down the coast new developments seemed to spring up daily.

The first hint that the sleeping beauty might awaken to become the Cinderella of the Gold Coast came in March 1925 when the *Palm Beach Post* reported the purchase of three-quarters of a mile of oceanfront

property by Rodman Wanamaker II. Wanamaker purchased the site in the interest of a syndicate of Palm Beach investors headed by the architect Addison Mizner. In the next month this group continued to quietly buy land until it had acquired about two miles of oceanfront property and an overall total of sixteen hundred acres.

Then on April 15, 1925, Mizner unveiled plans for a gigantic new development at Boca Raton. The Spanish-style Castillo del Rey, or King's Castle, a thousand-room, $6 million hotel on the oceanfront just north of the inlet anchored what Mizner called "the world's most architecturally beautiful playground." A casino, two golf courses designed by the well-known Donald Ross, a polo field, and miles of newly paved and lushly landscaped streets were only a few of the improvements the architect promised for the first year. Almost overnight Boca Raton had become Florida's "hottest" property.

Addison Mizner was born in Benicia, California, in 1872, the son of early pioneers of the state. Young Mizner first received his introduction to Spanish culture when President Benjamin Harrison appointed his father minister to the five Central American republics in 1889. Although Mizner had no formal university training in architecture, he studied design his entire life, beginning with the year in Guatemala and continuing for a short period at the University of Salamanca in Spain. Like most members of the profession of his era, Mizner received his formal training as an apprentice to a practicing architect. For almost three years in the mid-1890s he served in the

office of San Francisco architect Willis Polk, gaining his practical professional training.

Determined to become a society architect, Mizner opened a small office in New York City in 1904. Through childhood friends from San Francisco, Mrs. Hermann Oelrich and her sister, Mrs. William K. Vanderbilt II (they had been Tessie and Birdie Fair, daughters of the silver king James C. Fair), the young architect received the introductions and made the social contacts which helped to build his New York practice.

In 1907 Mizner received his first major commission, the completion of a partially finished collegiate Gothic townhouse for Stephen H. Brown, a stockbroker. During the next decade he received commissions for many houses on Long Island, an Adirondock camp, a stone mansion in Connecticut, and a small palace in Duchess County, New York. While stylistically an eclectic period, he produced Japanese houses and gardens, French Norman tennis pavilions, and "Alaskan mining towns," he also designed his first Spanish-style buildings. By the time Mizner arrived in Palm Beach in

January 1918, as the guest of sewing machine heir Paris Singer, he had both established himself in New York society and built a successful architectural career.

Mizner quickly gained the reputation as one of the nation's most prominent social architects. Beginning in 1918 with his design for Singer's Everglades Club, his Spanish and Italian-style buildings created an attractive and romantic alternative to the existing frame and shingle structures of the Flagler-era resort. Very quickly his architectural style found favor with Palm Beach's wealthiest and most fashionable.

After the architectural and social success of the Everglades Club, Mrs. Edward T. Stotesbury, wife of the Philadelphia banker and partner in J. P. Morgan and Company, asked Mizner to design her oceanfront villa, El Mirasol. As Palm Beach's reigning grande dame, Mrs. Stotesbury's commission confirmed the fashionableness of the new architectural style which now swept the resort.

This new architecture, often called the Palm Beach style, combined several elements. Mizner used handmade red barrel tiles for roofs, rough-textured

In 1925 the Mitchells constructed a large combination store, office, and apartment building which they called the Mitchell Arcade as it had open halls running both east and west as well as north and south on the first floor. It was located just south of Palmetto Park Road on the Dixie Highway. Floy Mitchell's first Boca Raton house had a kerosene stove, an icebox, a hand pump in the sink, and a "chick sale" in the backyard "with a cute half-moon cut out in the door." She was certainly thankful for the real estate boom and her new apartment with the modern kitchen and bathrooms it brought. While the Mitchells lived in one apartment and J.C. had his real estate office in part of the first floor, they were able to rent out the rest of the building. Until its new municipal building could be completed the town of Boca Raton rented office space in the arcade. This picture, taken around 1933, shows the recently

planted banyan tree that became a town landmark. In 1987 a fire gutted the building and then later in the year the county road department destroyed the tree to widen Dixie Highway.

stucco for walls, and for decorative detail wrought-iron grills and lighting fixtures, cast-stone window and door frames, arches, and columns. He made most of these products in his own workshops in West Palm Beach or imported them from Spain or Latin America. He also designed towers and many distinctive chimney pots on roofs to give his buildings a pronounced skyline and to project height, saying he found Florida "flat as a pancake." While Mizner preferred the Spanish Gothic period with its high-vaulted ceilings and elaborately detailed pointed arches for door and window frames, he borrowed freely from many Spanish periods and other Mediterranean countries, producing beautifully proportioned and tasteful buildings that remained distinctively his own creation.

At the same time, Mizner also realized that the hallmark of social architecture was its exclusiveness. Mizner designed his buildings to impress the neighbors, they never looked less expensive than they were. The air of antiquity of the architecture and the ancient imported one-of-a-kind furnishings—Mizner made yearly buying trips to Europe and returned with everything from staircases and fountains to tables and chairs, even to placemats and napkins—gave owners a

built-in sense of history that their own family trees often lacked. Very soon a Mizner mansion was seen as a short-cut to society. Certainly many of his clients thought their Mizner house had helped pave their way to social acceptance.

Finally, Mizner's unique contribution was combining personal architectural style and its exclusiveness with designs that aptly suited the lifestyles of his clients and the South Florida climate. As sports and informality ruled the daytime, Mizner's houses included relaxed and casual rooms with easy access to secluded patios, oceanfront terraces, swimming pools, and the beach. Convenient dressing rooms served those returning from water sports. Almost every house he designed contained a loggia which many see as the forerunner of the Florida and family rooms of a later day. His largest houses usually had a second loggia for breakfast and lunch.

The same houses adapted readily to the much more formal activities of the evening. Impressive entrance halls (the dressing rooms for beach users now served party guests), spacious drawing rooms with high-coffered ceilings and broad fireplaces, and equally impressive dining rooms, often with vaulted ceilings,

reached by a ceremonial route through hall and loggia from the drawing room produced a setting which added grandeur to even small occasions.

Mizner also recognized that the subtropical climate called for an architecture adapted to the sometimes intense heat. While earlier Palm Beach houses had verandahs overlooking ocean or lake, their rooms remained enclosed behind solid walls and small windows. Mizner opened his buildings to the out-of-doors. Masses of French doors or whole walls of windows that could slide into pockets, brought fresh air and cooling breezes into the house. He often designed principal rooms with three exposures and always used a plan only one room deep. High ceilings, arcaded cloisters on the south and west to shelter interior rooms from the hottest rays of the sun, cool tile floors, pools and trickling fountains, and masses of foliage, all produced a comfortable house in a hot climate.

Since 1918 Mizner had designed almost forty houses in the resort town. His clients included the brothers Charles and Gurnee Munn, Harold S. Vanderbilt, John S. Phipps and his brother Henry C. Phipps, Joseph M. Cudahy, Barclay Warburton, William Gray Warden, Edward and Paul Moore, Daniel Carstairs, Anthony J.

Drexel Biddle, Joseph Cosden, Edward Shearson, Dr. Preston Pope Satterwhite, William Wood, and Rodman Wanamaker II. Now many of these same people joined in the Boca Raton venture, becoming members of the syndicate which formed the Mizner Development Corporation. Other syndicate members included the Duchess of Sutherland, Paris Singer, Irving Berlin, W. K. Vanderbilt II, Madame Frances Alda, D. H. Conkling, W. C. Robinson, Porte Quinn, Elizabeth Arden, Clarence Geist, and T. Coleman du Pont. All were either well-known leaders of America's business, social, or entertainment fields or prominent local citizens who could help the project. Conkling published the *Palm Beach Post*, Quinn sold real estate. At the same time, several Boca Raton pioneers also invested in the Mizner company, hoping to prosper with the development of their community.

Harry Reichenbach, a high-powered New York press agent, was hired to direct the development's publicity. Within a week full-page advertisements for Boca Raton began to appear in both local and northern newspapers. From the beginning they emphasized the well-known people behind the Mizner organization, often giving the names of those who invested in Boca Raton and claiming they represented "considerably

Before Lafayette Cooke sold his Boca Raton property he reserved several lots for churches. As it was decided that the town could only support one congregation, the Community Church was built in 1925 on East Royal Palm Road where the NCNB Bank drive-in tellers are now located. Although called the Boca Raton Community Church, the little congregation was always served by Methodist clergymen. For the reception after the church dedication Floy Mitchell borrowed a zinc tub from Tony Brenk's store. Many of the guests became ill and Mrs. Mitchell later said, "That was how we learned never to make lemonade in a zinc tub."

over 1/3 of the entire wealth of the United States." At the same time the company advertisements always contained the hint that Boca Raton was a good investment and that land buyers could double or triple their purchase prices almost immediately.

The first offering of lots on May 14, 1925, saw "pandemonium" reigning in both the Miami and West Palm Beach offices. George Freyhofer, sales manager for the company, said Boca Raton had broken all first-day sales records with $2,100,000 in purchases. Two weeks later the company sold a further $2 million in lots at its second offering. By then Mizner had opened additional sales offices in New York City, Philadelphia, Pittsburgh, Chicago, and Boston.

Mizner's reputation convinced the Ritz-Carlton Investment Corporation, owner of the chain of elegant and exclusive hotels, to take over the Castillo del Rey on the ocean. As the Ritz-Carlton management planned to have Mizner's original hotel redesigned, he decided to immediately start construction on a small 100-room inn on the west shore of Lake Boca Raton. Every developer believed that a hotel lured potential land buyers to their project and Mizner was no exception. Karl Riddle, the project engineer, later claimed the harried architect ordered the new hotel staked out before he supplied the plans.

The publicity for Mizner's development also drew other real estate men who wished to become part of the action. Within a month several very large projects began taking form in Boca Raton. G. Frank Croissant, a Chicago developer, had come to Florida early in the boom. His first development, Croissant Park, was south of the New River in Fort Lauderdale. Using the same type of publicity as the other major Florida promoters he had sold out most of this subdivision when he decided to move north to Boca Raton. Croissant, who called himself "a builder of cities, not a subdivider," created the 2,360-acre Croissantania at prices "available to working men who could aid in the upbuilding of the entire community." Croissantania was west of Dixie

Highway and north of the Mizner lands. While Croissant's company released drawings for large hotels and other improvements, he started no building in the project.

By far the largest project to compete with Mizner was that of George W. Harvey of Boston. Harvey had already completed the fourteen-story Harvey Building in downtown West Palm Beach when he announced development of Villa Rica at Boca Raton. Planned as a complete 1,400-acre city completely within the boundaries of Boca Raton, Harvey told of $2 million in projects that included a Villa Rica Inn, a Florida East Coast Railway station, and a new post office. Harvey's company cleared and graded many acres of land, laid out and paved streets, and started construction of at least a dozen houses. This activity made Harvey Mizner's only real competitor and prompted many complaints from the Mizner Development Corporation.

Harvey's emphasis that Villa Rica was completely within the boundaries of Boca Raton might have been prompted by the subdivision of W. A. Mathes called Del Raton Park. Mathes, a West Palm Beach "developer and financier," said he planned to build an "American Venice." The large tract of land which he bought for $3 million was actually only a mile south of Atlantic Avenue and entirely within the city limits of Delray Beach. When this was pointed out to Mathes he said that although the project was in Delray Beach, "in physical and geographical features," it was identical with the "great Boca Raton subdivision which adjoins it on the South." While many developers used every means possible to draw people to their subdivisions, Mathes's unique gimmick was to form a symphony orchestra to give free concerts.

The summer and fall also saw many smaller subdivisions proposed for Boca Raton. Boca Highlands, Boca Raton Heights, and Boca Vista perhaps reassured the purchasers who feared finding their Florida land under water. Boca Vista claimed a location on the highlands of Boca Raton, thirty feet above sea level and "over-looking the entire city." Del Boca, Boca del Faro, Boca Centrale, and the Harley Gates sponsored projects, Kings Court, Kimberly Heights, and Elevado, quickly joined the list.

Wilson Mizner, Addison's younger brother, became an officer of the development company with the specific job of bringing entertainment to the new resort. His activity was an answer to the complaint that there was nothing to do in Florida at night. Wilson had authored several successful Broadway shows and had many contacts with the New York theatre world. According to him, although many New York productions wished to come to Florida, there were no adequate facilities in the state. To overcome this problem Addison designed a playhouse for Boca Raton. Wilson also purchased ships and barges with the plan to create the "Pirate Ship Cabaret" to be anchored in Lake Boca Raton. Wilson also said that Florenz Ziegfeld's successful *Palm Beach Nights,* produced in that resort, proved Florida's importance for the New York theatrical world. He promised more shows like *Palm Beach Nights* for Boca Raton. He also said the season would end in Boca Raton with a carnival "rivaling the New Orleans Mardi Gras." Since the development numbered Irving Berlin among its backers, his contribution to entertainment in Boca Raton could be taken for granted. The Mizner brothers also enlisted the comedienne Marie Dressler to come to Boca Raton. The new resort could both rival Palm

Addison Mizner was fifty-three years old in 1925 and at the height of his career as a Palm Beach social architect. He planned his new development in Boca Raton as the capstone to this already highly successful career, claiming his new resort would rival both Palm Beach and Coral Gables. To insure both its financial and social success his backers included noted businessmen and women and well-known socialites. Among these names appeared Harold and William K. Vanderbilt, J. Leonard Replogle, the Duchess of Sutherland, Paris Singer, Irving Berlin, Elizabeth Arden, Madame Frances Alda, Clarence H. Geist, T. Coleman du Pont, and Rodman Wanamaker II. The presumed support of these leaders of the nation's business, social and even entertainment worlds, plus the assurance that one of America's most creative architect's controlled its design, placed Boca Raton immediately in the forefront of the Florida boom-time development projects.

Beach in the entertainment it could attract, and according to Wilson, become a center that sent productions to northern stages.

As plans for the 160-foot wide Camino Real, the new inn on the lake, the Administration Buildings off Dixie Highway, the Spanish Village "large enough to hold much of the color and old world charm of those Spanish cities with which Mr. Mizner is familiar," a castle for Mizner on an island in Lake Boca Raton, and dozens of other projects went forward, so too did land sales. By the end of the summer of 1925 the company could claim $11 million worth of lots had been sold.

Although construction continued unabated into the fall, land sales in Boca Raton began to slow. Speculative booms, whether in real estate or the stockmarket, are based on confidence. The confidence that the buyer can sell his purchase at a profit in a constantly expanding market place. When the price rise slows, and when the market contracts, speculative booms collapse. Although the South Florida real estate market failed to see it at the time, the boom bubble was pricked as early as October 1925.

As the competition for land sales quickened over the summer, northern newspapers began carrying stories about "fraudulent misrepresentations" in the Florida market. All too often Florida promoters had sold land that flooded during the rainy season. Other developers had added "By-the-Sea" to their names even though they were located far inland. Northern investors who failed to inspect before buying often complained bitterly about these practices. Stories like these and many others found their way into print just as northern bankers, fearing the flow of capital from their banks to Florida, began warning their depositors about investing in Florida real estate.

Without question, many Florida developments were close to the line dividing legitimate from fraudulent. The Mizner organization realized this and decided to add a line to its advertisements to show the legitimacy of its promises: "attach this advertisement to your contract for deed. It becomes a part thereof." With this pledge the company hoped to both promote sales and counteract the attacks about dishonest Florida developments.

On April 15, 1925, Addison Mizner announced the start of a great scheme to build a new winter resort at Boca Raton. The first project, a $6 million oceanfront hotel called the Castillo del Rey, or "castle of the king," served as the anchor to the development and as a symbol to the architectural excellence and artistry of the new community. The 1,000-room hotel centered on an ornate Gothic entry which projected out from arcaded and balconied sections that connected the six- and seven-story wings. The asymmetrical design also included a high tower, vaguely modeled after the Giralda Tower in Seville.

The newspaper campaigns and the warnings of northern bankers did worry some investors. Unfortunately, during the summer other problems also surfaced for Florida's development. When the winter season ended in late April and early May, many Florida hotels, restaurants, and stores closed as few tourists braved the heat, humidity, and mosquitoes of a Florida summer. During the summer of 1925 many northerners decided to pile the family into the Model-T and see about the excitement in Florida. When they arrived they found shortages of hotel rooms which forced many to sleep in their cars or in hastily pitched tents. The visitors also found restaurants closed and fresh fruits and vegetables impossible to find. An ice shortage only added to their discomfort. Few of these summer visitors purchased real estate, and most spread the word about conditions in Florida when they returned north.

In order to prove that Mizner and the other developers intended to fulfill their promises they needed to continue construction of their projects. During the summer, first the Florida East Coast Railway, and then the Seaboard Air Line, imposed embargoes on all but perishable goods coming into South Florida. The railroads claimed they could find few employees to empty the cars when they arrived in South Florida. By summer 1925 the railroad yards in Miami, Fort Lauderdale, and West Palm Beach were jammed with fully loaded freight cars. With the entire south end of the peninsula dependent upon outside sources for building supplies, the embargo's effect on construction could quickly be seen.

T. Coleman du Pont served as chairman of the Mizner Development Corporation. T. Coleman, with his cousins Alfred and Pierre, had formed the modern E. I. du Pont de Nemours Company in 1902. Although he had left the company in 1915, he was still seen as one of the great financial geniuses of his era. His subsequent career in politics and his ownership of the Waldorf-Astoria Hotel had only added to the luster of his name. Many investors in Boca Raton real estate were encouraged by his association with the corporation.

The freight embargo which caused construction delays, the complaints of the summer tourists, the attacks by northern newspapers, and finally the bankers' warnings produced a climate that made Florida real estate a questionable investment for many people. Du Pont sensed this growing problem. He also realized that as chairman of the corporation, he might become personally responsible if the company failed to fulfill its many problems. He later claimed that he warned Reichenbach against placing the "attach this advertisement," statement to newspaper advertisements.

When the corporation board met in Palm Beach in October, du Pont resigned. He objected to the repeated use of his name in company advertisements, the campaign allowing buyers to attach advertisements to deeds, and in general the implication that he personally stood behind the company promises. When the Mizner

THE MOST FAMOUS HOTEL FOR THE GREATEST RESORT—BOCA RATON

Artist's conception of Ritz-Carlton Hotel as designed by Addison Mizner.

BOCA RATON HOTEL NEW LINK IN NOTED CHAIN

The Ritz-Carlton in Boca Raton will be the newest and most beautiful addition to the famous group of hotels under the same management, including the Carlton and Ritz Hotels of London—the Ritz of Paris—the Ritz of Madrid—the Esplanade of Berlin—the Esplanade of Hamburg—the National of Lucerne—the Excelsior of Rome—the Excelsior of Naples—the Splendide and the Royal at Evian les Bains—the Plaza at Buenos Aires, and Ritz-Carltons of Philadelphia, New York, Atlantic City, and Montreal.

To the better classes of Europe and to traveled Americans it is hardly necessary to describe the Ritz-Carlton Hotel system or to explain wherein its superiority lies. In a sense it is more than a system—it is a comprehensive plan combining organization, development and the features of centralized control and world-wide adaptability to the requirements of travelers of discrimination and refinement. As a hotel system it is the greatest in the world, with hotels upon three continents and in many countries.

MIZNER DEVELOPMENT CORPORATION
Main Office,
Palm Beach, Florida.
The resort city of unrivalled opportunity.

This full-page Mizner Development Corporation Advertisement appeared in the Palm Beach Post's *mid-summer edition. Advertisements for Boca Raton appeared regularly in most Florida newspapers and in many large northern cities. Emphasized in the advertisements were the projects planned for the resort, the individuals who had already purchased Boca Raton property, and how much the property values in the city had already risen. Within weeks after the announcement of the projected Castillo del Rey, Mizner reported that the Ritz-Carlton hotel chain had contracted to take over the building and running of the oceanfront hotel. This advertisement tells of the other major hotels in Paris, Madrid, Berlin, Rome, and London that are also part of the chain, and of the obvious pride that the development company takes in joining this illustrious company.*

corporation, realizing the possible consequences of his action, failed to announce the resignation, du Pont went to the *New York Times* in late November. He said differences between company officers and himself over what he saw as improper business methods forced his resignation. A few days later du Pont and several other members of the Mizner board who had also resigned said in a letter to the *Times* that they had almost no financial interest in the company and objected to the use of their names in advertisements for Boca Raton. One writer claimed that du Pont's letter "put a wet blanket on the entire boom." Certainly, the Mizner Development Corporation, which had sold over $25 million of Boca Raton real estate in just six months, was unable to survive du Pont's attack.

Although Mizner and the other South Florida developers attempted to fight back, October 1925 was the high point for sales and building permits. Company publicity noted that W. E. Shappercotter of the Lehigh Valley Railroad had assumed the chairmanship, and when any figure of prominence in financial circles visited Boca Raton they became evidence of the

continuing prosperity of the development. Company advertisements also emphasized the continuing building program. The completion of the Administration Building, the construction of a radio station "to broadcast the facts of Florida," the two thousand workers grading and paving streets, the plans for two hundred new houses, and the beginning of water and electrical service all became grist for the Reichenbach publicity mill.

Mizner also hurried construction of the Cloister Inn scheduled to open under Ritz-Carlton management. While the development company claimed the great oceanfront hotel's foundations would begin shortly, the Ritz-Carlton chain obviously had second thoughts about its Boca Raton investment. When the Ritz-Carlton Cloister Inn did open on February 6, 1926, it was evident that the land boom had ended. While the publicity department could continue to discuss the $10,000-a-room furnishings of the Inn and quoted Stanford White's widow's reaction to the hotel: "This building is superb," buyers for Boca Raton real estate could no longer be found.

THE CLOISTE[R]

Even before the first lots could be offered for sale, in Boca Raton the Ritz-Carlton Investment Corporation agreed to build a new Ritz-Carlton hotel on the beachfront in place of Mizner's Castillo del Rey. As the Ritz-Carlton hotel would be smaller and more luxurious than Mizner's planned hotel and would take longer to design and build, Mizner announced that his corporation would build immediately a small, 100-room inn on the west side of Lake Boca Raton. The waterfront site of the Cloister Inn inspired the many Venetian architectural motifs found in its design.

Although the company claimed it sold $6 million of property over the winter season, sales by spring had almost completely ended. Moreover, many earlier purchasers of land now had second installments due. Many, of course, had bought only for speculation and planned to sell their lots at a profit long before the second payment was required. All too often these investors found by late fall 1925 that they rarely could sell at a profit, and often could find no buyer. Many thought they had made an unwise investment and decided to withhold the second payment. As Mizner needed the continuing flow of money from the yearly time payments as well as infusions of capital from new purchasers to continue his many projects, by spring Boca Raton construction came largely to a standstill.

By April the company was unable to meet payments on promissory notes signed to purchase land in Boca Raton. When various contractors found Mizner had no money to pay bills they began filing liens against the corporation. With these financial problems, Mizner's backers demanded the company be reorganized. In July,

the Chicago-based Central Equities Corporation of Rufus Dawes and his brother, United States Vice President Charles Dawes, assumed management of the company.

The boom had ended and projects all over South Florida faced bankruptcy. The Dawes brothers found they were unable to reverse the fortunes of Boca Raton. When the great hurricane of September 1926 hit the southern tip of the state causing both loss of life and much physical destruction, the Dawes brothers gave up, and the failed Mizner Development Corporation also faced the bankruptcy courts.

Boca Raton had entered the 1920s a small unincorporated farming village with only a few hundred pioneer residents. The land boom of the era, and the interest of Addison Mizner, made it one of the best known cities of Florida by the end of the decade. While critics of Mizner's development company point to its failure, for Boca Raton the company's activities meant buildings, jobs, and permanent residents. Boca Raton would never slip back into that early obscurity.

These Boca Raton buses are parked before the Via Mizner on Worth Avenue in Palm Beach. The Pullman buses purchased by the Mizner Development Corporation carried prospective purchasers to see the wonders being worked in Boca Raton. The battleship-gray buses with Boca Raton lettered in deep red, had wicker seats for the passengers' comfort. Buses ran from company offices on Flagler Street in Miami and from its headquarters in Palm Beach. Addison Mizner's own apartment can be seen on the second floor to the left. His office and the development company's headquarters are on the right. Wilson Mizner, the architect's brother and vice-president of the development company, stands in white shirt and trousers in the center of a group of company salesmen.

Most of the large South Florida developers like Fisher, Merrick, and Young established offices on East Flagler Street in Miami. Naturally the Mizner Development Corporation believed it needed an office on the street, already crowded with real estate dealers. In order to attain this preferred address the company was forced to pay $275,000 to acquire a 99-year lease on a building housing a restaurant. Although the Mizner corporation spent thousands of dollars to convert Ye Wayside Inn at 133 East Flagler Street into a magnificent Spanish-style showcase, the company's salesmen moved in immediately, taking over the restaurant's tables for their desks.

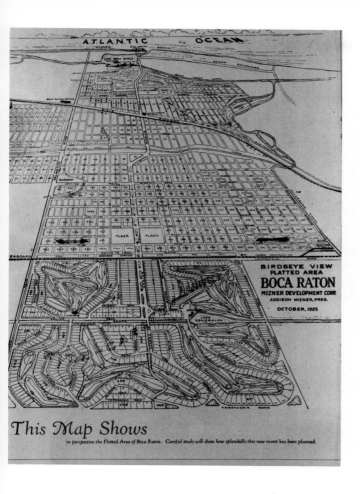

In late May 1925 the Boca Raton Council appointed Mizner town planner. This allowed Mizner and his staff to plat both the land of the development company and the rest of the unplatted land within the city limits. Under the new plan the 160-foot-wide Camino Real became the city's principal east-west street. The new street began at the Ritz-Carlton hotel on the beach and crossed the East Coast Canal on a Venetian bridge Mizner designed. The elaborately detailed bridge included a tower with an apartment for the bridgekeeper. After passing through the Cloister Inn golf course, Camino Real became the shopping street for the new resort. Mizner planned to build several store-office-apartment complexes similar to the Via Mizner and Via Parigi in Palm Beach. This section of the street had a central canal modeled on the Botofago of Rio de Janeiro. In traveling west the street continued through residential areas to a great plaza centered on the proposed Seaboard Railway station. Camino Real ended in the midst of the meandering streets of Ritz-Carlton Park, two-and-a-half miles from the ocean.

Mizner believed that a hotel was necessary to lure potential real estate investors and to make the development a success. Consequently he rushed construction of the Cloister Inn. In his haste to start building he ordered the site staked out. This forced his engineer to remind him that he first needed the dimensions and foundation plans. Nonetheless, the structure, built of hollow tile walls, rose rapidly once plans were supplied.

Every boom-time development in Florida had a full-time publicity department on its payroll. Practically every newspaper and magazine article about Boca Raton came from the pen of Harry Reichenbach, publicity director for the Mizner interests. A January 1926 article proclaimed Lake Boca Raton as the new rival to Italy's Lake Como and Lakes Chillon and Lucern in Switzerland. "Lake Boca Raton will possess a quality of beauty that will recommend it to the same praise." After dredging the little lake, Mizner planned to install "Venetian type" bulkheading. Then "Lazy gondolas," "great white-winged sailboats," and "pinkish winged Flamingos" could join the deepwater yachts floating across the lake to view the area's tropical beauty.

This aerial view of the Cloister Inn shows the dredging of Lake Boca Raton and the new golf course under construction. As the construction of the hotel proceeded, so did the dredging and bulkheading of Lake Boca Raton. Mizner's plans called for a large yacht basin and a deep inlet. At the same time land was cleared and fairways and greens constructed for the golf course designed by Donald Ross for the hotel.

RESIDENCE OF ADDISON MIZNER AT LAKE BOCA RATON
THE ENTRANCE ACROSS THE DRAWBRIDGE INTO THE FOREi CURT

When Harry Reichenbach released sketches of Mizner's castle, on an island in the northern part of Lake Boca Raton, he said it would create a picture artists would "reproduce the world over on canvas and by photograph." For the design the architect said he envisioned "a Spanish fortress of the twelfth century captured from its owner by a stronger enemy, who, after taking it, adds on one wing and another . . . ." The castle included a working drawbridge, a dining room with panels from the room in which Ferdinand and Isabella issued Columbus's final instructions before he departed for America, and a 36-by-52-foot living room, even larger and more beautiful than that in his Palm Beach apartment. The architect planned to spend over a million dollars for his castle which after his death he pledged to the city of Boca Raton for a museum.

The Villa Lucinda was one of many proposed mansions for Boca Raton. The Mizner company's publicity office quickly announced that many of the architect's backers and former Palm Beach clients wished to build large Mizner-designed residences in Boca Raton. The Joshua Cosdens, who had commissioned Mizner's largest Palm Beach villa, Playa Riente, had recently sold it to Mrs. Horace Dodge, widow of the automobile maker, for $2.8 million. Reports from the publicity office claimed that Nell Cosden had asked Mizner to start work on a new Boca Raton mansion to equal the old in size and elegance. Other clients for whom the architect also completed elaborate plans in the new resort included the opera star Madame Frances Alda; Dr. Maurice Druker, who planned to build a large subdivision in the city; Anderson T. Herd, a development company executive; and A. S. Alexander, a Palm Beach socialite. While Mizner could claim that the wealthy and socially prominent supported Boca Raton, he also projected moderately priced subdivisions for his resort city.

Architect's sketches of proposed houses for Old Floresta were published in a development brochure. Mizner proposed to build at least one hundred houses in the Old Floresta subdivision. He designed ten different models which he designated "A" through "J" and then planned to site them so that no street had more than one house, or its mirror image, of the same plan. The twenty-nine houses actually built represented only a fraction of those originally planned. The Dwight P. Robinson Company, the New York firm building the Cloister Inn, started construction of the houses in October 1925. The houses pictured in a Mizner Development company advertisement are all large two-story models with three bedrooms and two baths. Each had large screened porches and sleeping porches or open decks on the second floor. Even the smallest one-bedroom Old Floresta houses had exceptionally large living rooms with fireplaces, and many windows to capture every breeze.

This view of western Palmetto Park Road in the 1920s looks east from near today's Fourth Avenue. The isolated lane connected Mizner's small twenty-nine house community, later named Old Floresta, with downtown Boca Raton and the Dixie Highway. Mizner's plans for the road called for making it one of the major east-west streets of Boca Raton and extending far to the west to his golf course community of Ritz-Carlton Park. Like Camino Real, Palmetto Park Road was also to have a central canal dividing lanes of traffic as it moved west from the downtown area.
Historical Society of Palm Beach County

Addison Mizner designed one Old Floresta house especially for his brother, the Reverend Henry W. Mizner, who planned to retire in Boca Raton after twenty-five years service as head of St. Stephen's House, an Episcopal mission and church on the near southside of St. Louis. Father Mizner had originally entered West Point to prepare for a military career. The example of an Episcopal priest who lost his life caring for victims of a yellow fever epidemic changed his mind about the Army. In his fourth year at West Point he resigned and entered the General Theological Seminary in New York.

Father Mizner's health had been poor for several years. When his mother-in-law died and left his family a small yearly income he decided to retire to his brother's new Florida community. Mizner, his wife, the former Margot Alice Postlewaite, and their young daughter Alice arrived in June 1926. Their house on Oleander Street received special attention from Addison Mizner who added a molded Spanish-Colonial door surround, several bull's-eye windows, and many French doors opening on wrought-iron balconies. The interior included hand stenciled decoration on the ornate pecky cypress ceiling of the living room, a study for the clergyman, a large formal dining room, and while many Old Floresta kitchens could fit into a closet, this one was full-sized with eating space. A newspaper article of the period mentioned that Henry Mizner planted many rare tropical plants and trees, and placed antique busts and urns around his house giving the property "a real old world appearance."

As Father Mizner wished to remain active in his retirement, Addison Mizner fitted out an old surveyor's hut as a small frame chapel for Boca Raton's Episcopal community. Located on South Dixie Highway, just north of Camino Real, little St. Mary's Chapel contained one long room protected by a full-length porch. The small building, no longer being used as a church, was swept away in the 1928 hurricane.

Father Mizner and children from the church school are seated on the steps of St. Mary's Episcopal Chapel. The photograph is inscribed on the reverse: "To Imogene from Father Mizner." Imogene Gates, who is seen on the far left of the top row, was the daughter of Harley. Her brother Buddy is seated directly in front of her. The little boy who's head is circled was named Junior.

The interior of St. Mary's Episcopal Chapel is decorated for Easter service in 1927. Although Father Mizner conducted services in Boca Raton for almost a year, Bishop Cameron Mann of South Florida refused to accept his transfer to the Diocese, claiming Mizner had not been called to a specific parish. On the evening the new Ritz-Carlton Cloister Inn opened in February 1926, Addison Mizner tried to overcome this difficulty by announcing plans to build a great church in Boca Raton dedicated to the memory of the brothers' mother. Obviously, the new parish would choose the Reverend Henry Mizner as its rector. The end of the boom also ended plans for the new church. When former owners of the Old Floresta land foreclosed on their mortgage, Henry Mizner and his family moved to Paris, where he died on July 8, 1930.

Addison Mizner designed this new station for the Florida East Coast Railway for a location near Palmetto Park Road and Dixie Highway. The high imposing tower, capped by a wrought-iron weathervane, and the monumental plaza with its elaborate fountain would certainly have given passengers a sense of arriving at some place very special. Unfortunately, the bust came before the station could be built.

In January 1926 Mizner released sketches for a large two-story City Hall for Boca Raton. The town planned to pay for the elegantly detailed new building with the greatly increased revenues generated by real estate taxes. By the time Mizner had finished his plans, town officials realized that the boom had ended and that they could no longer afford the large new building. At first Mizner scaled down his plans by eliminating the second floor and the southern wing. Although Mizner continued his interest in the new City Hall until the fall of 1926, William E. Alsmeyer, a Delray Beach architect, took charge of the construction and added a small second story under the pitched roof of the building's main section and a garage for the fire engine. Mizner's designs for stone work, ornamental grills, electrical fixtures, and other architectural details remained a part of the completed building. The Library of Congress

The small Boca Raton sales office for George Harvey's Villa Rica was built on Dixie Highway. When the Mizner plans for Boca Raton gained national attention, other developers quickly announced their own subdivisions in the south county area. Some, like Croissantania, the 2,360-acre tract of Chicago promoter G. Frank Croissant almost equalled the Mizner development in scale. Others like Boca Vista, on the highlands of the city, thirty feet above sea level, and Boca Centrale, in the heart of downtown, consisted of only a few lots. Among the largest, Villa Rica rivaled the Mizner company in its promotions and national publicity. The Villa Rica sign advertises ocean, lake, and canal residential lots on easy terms. On the right are the Florida East Coast Railway tracks and the almost deserted Dixie Highway which Harvey promised to widen to ninety feet through his property.

George W. Harvey, a real estate man who had first come to prominence in Boston, arrived in West Palm Beach early in the boom period. In that city he constructed the fourteen-story Harvey Building, its highest "skyscraper." He now proposed to spend $2 million on the Villa Rica subdivision. Like Mizner, he believed a hotel necessary to attract prospective purchasers of his real estate. Harvey thought the Spanish-style Villa Rica Inn, designed by Delray architect Sam Ogren, and to cost $500,000, would rival Mizner's Cloister Inn. The three-story, 100-room hotel, planned for a site overlooking the shores of the "pretty little lake in Villa Rica" near today's Spanish River Boulevard, was never built.

Since Harvey envisioned a complete 1,400-acre modern city he proposed a new $25,000 Florida East Coast Railway passenger station designed by Sam Ogren for his property. The long low Spanish-style station was to be built just off the Dixie Highway. While many of the small Boca Raton developments purchased land from Mizner's company and looked to his design standards for their projects, the Palm Beach architect saw George Harvey as an unwanted competitor. When the sketch for the Villa Rica station appeared in the Palm Beach Post on November 8, 1925, Mizner protested to the railway company, claiming there could only be one Boca Raton station.

Mizner also complained when he saw the Sam Ogren drawing for a proposed Boca Raton post office located in Villa Rica. While technically within the incorporated area of Boca Raton, Villa Rica was two miles north of Palmetto Park Road. For residents accustomed to daily visits to the post office to pick up mail and trade gossip, the location seemed most inconvenient.

As the Villa Rica houses neared completion, Harvey found his company had difficulty selling lots in the project. At this time Mizner also began experiencing difficulties. Mizner's publicity told of the interest of New York banker Otto Kahn in his project as well as Charles M. Schwab, one of the organizers of United States Steel. Charles Merrick had hired former Democratic presidential candidate and Secretary of State William Jennings Bryan to help sell Coral Gables. Harvey, as a Bostonian, called upon longtime Boston Mayor James M. Curley, at many times his salary as mayor, to promote Villa Rica.

Many boom-time developers had no intention of fulfilling the many promises they made in their advertisements. Constructing roads, laying water mains, installing streetlights, and building hotels and houses called for heavy investments. Many developers neither had the money nor wished to go to the trouble of completing their subdivisions. They just planned to sell off the lots—with buyers often choosing from maps in the company offices—and pocket their profits. Both Mizner and George Harvey made a conscientious effort to complete their projects. The stock piles of lumber at Villa Rica is evidence of Harvey's commitment.

George Harvey's Villa Rica extended from Dixie Highway to the ocean. Although the company planned a bridge to be "a thing of beauty and strictly in keeping with the general dignity" of all Villa Rica work, the county built a standard drawbridge over the East Coast canal to furnish access to the beach for the subdivision. The bridge, near the current Spanish River Boulevard bridge, was later moved to another location after Villa Rica's failure. Harvey also meant for this street, called Ocean Avenue, to be a ninety-foot wide boulevard. While the several miles of paved streets remained a monument to Harvey's efforts for many years, the hurricane of 1926 wrecked most of the houses constructed in the subdivision.

The large two-story houses built in Villa Rica were typical of Spanish-influenced tract housing of the era. Harvey constructed these vaguely mission-style houses with their stucco walls, barrel-tiled sun shades, and scalloped parapets just off Dixie Highway on a section of cleared land with gravel-paved streets. Company publicity said that all houses built in Villa Rica had to conform to either the Spanish style or "Spanish and Venetian" styles. These restrictions "insure a class of buildings that will be a credit to the city." Harley Gates later said Harvey completed a dozen houses and a tea room on what today is North Federal Highway.

Villa Rica workers, housed in a temporary shantytown to the west of Dixie Highway, came from all over the eastern United States. While Mizner built temporary dormitories and apartments to house the white engineers and supervisors of his project, day-labor was scare and either had to travel from as far away as West Palm Beach or be content with the shack camps squatting on vacant land.

Karl Riddle assembled a large staff of engineers and surveyors to meet the requirements of the Boca Raton development. While Mizner might have the official title of town planner, his professional engineers and surveyors carried out the actual platting. Most of the new town conformed to the grid system of squared blocks with twenty-five to fifty-foot lots so common to South Florida boom-time developments. Riddle, a trained professional engineer, later served as city manager and mayor of West Palm Beach and first engineer of Palm Beach County.

Construction started on the northern Administration Building located at the corner of Dixie Highway and Camino Real in early May 1925. It was designed by Mizner to house the offices of his sales staff. He modeled the building after the house of artist El Greco in Toledo, Spain. On this, the Camino Real facade, Mizner used a simplified Spanish-baroque door surround broken by a second-story balconied French door. The massive entrance doors were studded with metal rosettes. Some first-floor windows were protected by crudely fabricated wrought-iron grills.

The northern Administration Building surrounded a paved patio with a small polychromed tile fountain at its center. A covered walkway on the east side, formed by the overhang of the second-floor gallery, was supported by two squared cast-concrete Moresque columns and a gigantic pecky cypress beam. Mizner's design for the patio is particularly faithful to that of the El Greco house. He even installed large iron rings near the roof line on the east and west sides like the awning supports in the El Greco patio.

The south facade of the northern Administration Building also shows many similarities to the El Greco garden front. The porch with its columns with cannon ball capitals, the covered entrance to the patio, and the series of three rounded windows all faithfully reproduce the Toledo house. As headquarters for the sales force the beautiful detailing of the northern building allowed the prospective land purchaser to see the elegance planned for the future resort.

Mizner Industries, the architect's workshops and factories in West Palm Beach, made the wrought-iron grills used on the windows of the northern Administration Building. As each grill was handmade, each was different.

In December 1925 the northern Administration Building opened for lunch and tea, served on the porch and patio. Peter Larsen, owner of the fashionable Patio Restaurant in Palm Beach's Via Mizner operated the new facility for the development company. Addison Mizner, in white, is shown in this Palm Beach Post *photograph having luncheon with friends on the porch. While a large professional kitchen was later installed in the northwest wing of the southern Administration Building, the northern building contained a reproduction of El Greco's small colorfully tiled kitchen.*

Mizner rushed the southern Administration Building to completion to house Riddle's large engineering staff. This courtyard view shows the first-floor colonade with the capitals matching those on the northern building and the row of windows on the second floor marking the skylighted drafting room. Harry Vought and Company, with offices in New York City and Palm Beach, received the contract to construct the southern building. Vought also built a series of Mizner-designed bungalows in a section of Boca Raton later called Spanish Village. Although he planned to construct over one hundred houses, he finished less than twenty of the modest two-bedroom bungalows which originally sold for $7,250.

By the end of October 1925 the Mizner company reported that over two thousand workers were leveling and grading the streets in the new development. Although the location of this street making activity is unknown, the photograph does show the heavily wooded conditions found in Boca Raton in the 1920s.

Florida State Archives

One critic remarked that the western, or entrance front of the Ritz-Carlton Cloister Inn seemed like an isolated convent on the Spanish plains. Addison Mizner and his development company hosted a great society dinner of February 7, 1926, to mark the grand opening of the hotel. The publicity releases said that the guest list rivaled the social registers of two continents. "Red-coated, gold-braided servitors, responding in French and Spanish to whispered queries; delicious viands, piping hot, wonderfully seasoned and beautifully served, made this a truly Lucullan repast." Alexander P. Moore, formerly United States ambassador to Spain, called Mizner "the Michael Angelo of America," saying his hotel was the finest piece of architecture in the country.

The high-arched loggia of the Ritz-Carlton Cloister Inn led to the lounge and dining hall. One description of the hotel said the little balconies off the second-floor bedrooms "invite serenaders." On opening night Grant Clarke, "official lyricist of Boca Raton," played his new tango entitled "Boca Raton." Clarke, noted for his early work such as "Get Out and Get Under," and "Secondhand Rose," captured the speculative quality of the Mizner Development Corporation in one verse of his new song: "Think of old Captain Kidd / Think of a chest that he hid / Dream that you've opened the lid / You're in Boca Raton."

Mizner modeled the Ritz-Carlton Cloister Inn dining hall upon a fifteenth-century hospital at Vich in Catalonia. A press release said the feeling of the old hospital was perpetuated in the five arched bays supporting a ceiling of beams and sapling poles. Along the walls were placed Spanish lavabos. These washstands were used by diners in ancient times to wash the "fat foods" from their hands after eating. The tables and nail-studded leather chairs, wrought-iron chandeliers and candle holders, tile floors, cast-stone window surrounds, and even the stained-glass windows in tones of "aquamarine, sapphire, and azure," were all products of Mizner's workshops in West Palm Beach.

One entered the lofty forty-foot-square lobby through gigantic ancient Spanish wooden doors. The severity of the two-story-high plaster walls was broken only by the wooden balcony on two sides on the second floor. "The ancient handrail" on the balustrade, according to one writer, "carries the imagination back to those medieval days when handrails were hewn out of slender logs." A great Spanish lantern hanging in the center of the lobby and a red tile floor completed the picture of restrained elegance.

70

The Cloister Inn, completed at a cost of $1,250,000, has been called the most expensive 100-room hotel ever built. Mizner made most of the furnishings of the inn at his workshops in West Palm Beach. Here in the smoking room can be seen the austerity and simplicity of furnishings often mentioned in reports on the hotel. All the furnishings are from Mizner Industries including the large upholstered "Papa Mizner" chair in the corner and even the pottery and wrought-iron lamps on the writing table. This simplicity was also maintained in the bedrooms where the walls were a "creamy whitewash," while the shutters, doors, and bedspreads were a "curious tomato color." The beds themselves were hand painted with antique Spanish designs.

The workshops of Mizner Industries were located on Bunker Road in West Palm Beach. He began by making roof tiles as he said the standard American tiles had the color of a "slaughter house floor." As he called his tile factory Los Manos—or handmade—the myth grew up that his workers molded the barrel tiles on their thighs. In reality they used wooden molds. Over the years Mizner added more workshops to the gigantic operation that became Mizner Industries. His furniture workshops became necessary when he needed more Spanish furniture to decorate his houses than he could import. The workers are finishing the writing tables and bedside stands found in the Cloister Inn guest rooms.
Historical Society of Palm Beach County

One critic called the raftered great hall of the Cloister Inn its loveliest room. On cool nights logs burned in the huge fireplace with its Mizner Industries cast-stone mantle topped by an immense royal banner. Around the room shields placed high on the walls held clusters of brightly colored Spanish flags. The room almost projects out over the lake, causing one writer to claim he had the sensation of being on a boat, "resting upon blue and green tropical waters." Those colors were repeated in the stained glass of the windows.

On Christmas Eve 1925 Mizner hosted a small dinner at the still unfinished Cloister Inn for a few friends and former clients. At this time he announced that the Ritz-Carlton organization had agreed to assume management of the hotel when it opened in February. Standing are Albert Keller, manager of the New York City Ritz-Carlton; Addison and Wilson Mizner; Gustave Toff, new manager of the Ritz-Carlton Cloister Inn; and seated is Henri Prince, assistant manager of the Inn.

The Boca Raton Hunt Club was organized in January 1927 with a charter membership of sixty. The club provided facilities for riding, hunting, fishing, and other sports according to Harley Gates in Boca Ratone, Florida: A Romance of the Past, A Vision of the Future. He also claimed the club had twenty good saddle horses and a hunting lodge at its disposal. Clint Moore, who came to Boca Raton from Tennessee to pave the streets in Mizner's development, brought many of the horses with him.

Wilson and Addison Mizner were photographed with Marie Dressler, who during the boom period was often called "the duchess of Boca Raton." By 1925 Dressler's Broadway career as a comedienne was at a standstill. A friend of both Mizner brothers, she was invited to come to Boca Raton and help sell real estate. In leaving New York she told a reporter, "I warn you I'm going to be a successful real estate dealer. I'm mad about Florida. I'm not afraid of work." How much, if any, real estate she sold is unknown. Certainly her name was an asset for the development company and many people stopped in the Boca Raton offices for a chance to meet her. After the bust she returned to acting, gaining a second very successful career in film. When she wrote her autobiography she had forgotten that the Mizners had given her a job when she needed one and only remembered that she had been used by them to advertise Boca Raton.

After the February opening of the new hotel the social columns of the Palm Beach newspapers detailed the daily trips to the south county of the socialite friends and former clients of the architect. Before the end of the month, Mizner's publicity agents could also report that Charles Ritz, son of the founder of the hotel chain, and his new bride were spending a belated honeymoon at the Inn. Other visitors included Sgt. Alvin C. York, the World War I hero, who stayed at the hotel while fundraising for a school in the Tennessee mountains. While it was evident the rich and powerful approved of the small Inn, the longtime residents of Boca Raton probably enjoyed the new facility even more. Helen Howard and Harriette Gates are seated on Mizner Industries' wicker chairs in the cloister overlooking Lake Boca Raton.

Although Carl Fisher's wife Jane had already posed in what at the time was considered a daring one-piece bathing suit, the Mizner organization received wide publicity when it sent out this photograph of a former "Miss Alaska" on the Boca Raton beach with her "bubble machine."

Harley Gates returned to Boca Raton during the land boom period, and built this residence in the Spanish style on South Federal Highway at the corner of Third Street. The small house served both as the office for his real estate business and as the location of his wife's antiques store. The 1927 building with its colorful Spanish tiles was demolished in 1959 to make way for the Royal Palm Plaza shopping center.

Although the new Town Hall had a garage specifically designed for the use of the fire truck, in July 1928, Mayor John Brown wrote to Chief Guy J. Bender ordering him "to immediately bring the engine and equipment over to the fire station," as the Town Commission had decided it must be stored in the fire hall. Perhaps Chief Bender had driven Old Betsy home at night. If so, the problem soon ended when the commission allowed a small apartment to be created on the second floor of Town Hall for the chief and his family. This photograph shows the new Town Hall, Old Betsy, the volunteer fire department, and Chief Bender on the far right.

G.J. BENDER, CHIEF.
M.W STOKES — ASST CHIEF
JOHN LA MONT, DRIVER. BOCA RA
HARRY PURDOM. ASST DRIVER.
J.K. Mc CLINTOCK, CAP
E.M. THOMASON

In April 1926 Boca Raton paid $12,500 for the American-LaFrance fire engine that has since been known as Old Betsy. The town made a $1,000 down payment and executed three $3,833.34 notes, payable each year for the next three years. Although the fire engine was quickly delivered and placed into use, when the first note came due in April 1927 the boom had ended and the town had no money. Over the next few years a very tolerant American-LaFrance company allowed Boca Raton to make greatly scaled-down payments. A 1926 ordinance established a volunteer fire department with a "chief of fire" to be paid $12.50 a month,

an assistant chief at $8.00, and a driver at $5.00. The chief of fire could appoint up to twelve firemen who were paid $4.00 per fire and $2.00 per drill. Old Betsy, the new town hall, and the volunteer fire department are seen in this photograph of August 1927. From left to right are Strout Eldredge; M. W. Stokes, assistant chief; O. Ozier; John LaMont, driver; Harry Purdom, assistant driver; Guy J. Bender, chief of fire; O. Arnold; Sam Jenkins; F. M. Thomason; Kline Platt; and J. K. McClintock, captain.

With the incorporation of the town of Boca Raton and the coming of the Mizner boom, town fathers found it necessary to formally provide for police and fire protection for their citizens. An emergency ordinance of September 23, 1925, appointed Charles J. Raulerson, seen here on the left, as first town marshall at a salary of $175 per month. On the right is Leo Godwin, deputy marshall. An audit statement for the police department for the year ending October 3, 1926, included one Ford touring car, also seen in the photograph, two Henderson motorcycles, five revolvers, and three pairs of handcuffs, all property valued at $1,639.68. When a later audit found that the police department had used eighty-five gallons of gas in seventeen days, Mayor John G. Brown threatened to discontinue the use of the Ford.

By the time the Ritz-Carlton Cloister Inn opened the town police force had grown to five members. Seen here from left to right are Marshall Ira Blackman (on the Henderson motorcycle), Dan Kenneff, Rufus White, Charles Raulerson, and Leo Godwin. As it became obvious the boom had ended, the town was forced to cut down the number of men on the force. As early as October 1928 the City Council questioned whether it could continue to maintain a police department. Finally, when Ira Blackman resigned in September 1929, Boca Raton lost its last police officer. This prompted the mayor to ask Palm Beach County Sheriff R. C. Baker if he could supply an experienced deputy to police the city during the winter season.

While the Mizner Development Corporation's bankruptcy created many problems for the town, the Chamber of Commerce decided to continue its promotions. When the Shriners held their national convention in Miami, the Chamber decided to boost Boca Raton. J. C. Mitchell appealed to the Town Council on April 4, 1928, for $1,000 to construct a giant wooden camel, symbol of the Shriners, across Dixie Highway, just north of Palmetto Park Road. Since any member of the lodge who drove to Miami would be forced to take Dixie Highway, all would pass under the camel, and the chamber argued, carry the name of Boca Raton across the country. The council agreed to the idea on April 9, and by the end of the month J. F. Cramer of Cramer and Cramer had erected the camel.

When the Town Council approved the money to build the camel, the Elks Club decided that they also needed publicity and were able to find $540 to transform the two-by-four and beaverboard beast into something at least resembling an elk. When the last Shriner passed under the camel, its hump disappeared and strange horns sprouted from its head. Thus when the Elks met in Miami in July, they also could pass under a giant symbol of their organization.

Clarence Geist's Palm Beach villa on Golf View Road occupied a commanding position just to the east of the exclusive Everglades Club House. Designed by Marion Sims Wyeth, one of the resorts most fashionable architects, the towered Spanish-style house was erected in 1924. Although myth claimed that the Everglades Club membership committee blackballed Geist's application, he became a member early in the 1920s. Harold L. Ickes, secretary of the interior under President Franklin Roosevelt, called Geist an "exceedingly rough diamond." Nonetheless, despite his "practised poor manners," the utilities magnate regularly "hobnobbed" with some of the country's most influential and wealthy people.

C H A P T E R   III

THE GEIST ERA

Late in April 1927 Boca Raton pioneers Harry and Ethel Chesebro filed suit in Palm Beach County Courts asking for the recovery of property sold in 1925 to the Mizner Development Corporation. The Chesebros claimed that Mizner was in arrears in payments for both principal and interest and owed the balance of $75,000. They asked the court to sell the property to satisfy the outstanding debt. The 32-acre site contained the jewel of the development company's Boca Raton holdings, the Ritz-Carlton Cloister Inn.

In March, Judge C. E. Chillingworth ordered Mizner's company to pay over $40,000 to the former owners of the 255-acre tract west of the downtown where the architect built twenty-nine houses. Some of this money was designated for the suppliers of materials for these houses. Judge Chillingworth also appointed a special master in chancery to sell the property should the Mizner Corporation fail to satisfy the debt.

The Chesebro suit, in which a number of other individuals and companies still owed money for services and materials supplied for the hotel joined, was the final recognition of the Mizner Development Corporation's bankruptcy. The court now lumped together all the remaining Mizner properties east of the Florida East Coast Railway tracks and appointed three trustees in bankruptcy to dispose of the company's assets.

In October, Jerome D. Gedney, a New York City attorney, bid $5,000 and offered to assume the outstanding debts of between $10 million and $15 million for the 15,000-acre holdings which included the inn, the administration buildings, and a number of houses. At the same time, M. Specktor, a West Palm Beach furniture dealer, bid $28,000 for the hotel's furnishings. When one of the trustees objected, claiming the bids were to low, the court's referee in bankruptcy rejected both bids.

At the end of a second round of bidding on November 1, 1927, Gedney raised his offer to $71,500. Although Gedney said he represented a secret client, within days, Clarence H. Geist revealed his interest in the project. Geist, a Philadelphia utilities magnate, had been an original investor in the Mizner Development Corporation. Both the trustees and the referee accepted Geist's bid, pointing out that he planned to carry on the Mizner development, although "in an adjusted form." The trustees also scaled down their estimate of the overall debt to approximately $7 million.

Clarence H. Geist, born on a LaPorte, Indiana farm in 1866, went west after his education at Valparaiso Normal School. For several years he roamed the country dealing in livestock, "principally horses, and living largely in the saddle." He later said that he returned to Chicago because "no one in the West had any money and I discovered the fact that I could not make any money where there wasn't any." After working for the Rock Island Railroad he entered the real estate business. During this period he

The dining room in Clarence Geist's Palm Beach house served as the setting for many "charming and beautifully appointed" parties given by the Geists. One source says Geist was "an extrovert who enjoyed entertaining, enjoyed games, and enjoyed people." The Palm Beach Post *called the villa "one of the most beautifully furnished of the period houses" in the resort. The dining room's decoration combined Spanish antiques and reproductions manufactured by Mizner Industries in West Palm Beach. Both the floor tiles and the cast mantle were also products of Mizner's workshops.*

also became associated with Rufus and Charles G. Dawes in the development of gas and electric utilities companies.

In 1905 Geist married Florence Hewitt of Philadelphia and moved east to her city. While he and the Dawes brothers retained their interest in midwestern utility companies until the 1920s when they sold their holdings to the Samuel Insull group, Geist began investing in eastern utilities after 1905. He controlled the Philadelphia Suburban Water Company, which supplied forty-nine eastern Pennsylvania towns, and was the largest stockholder in the United Gas Improvement Company, a Philadelphia holding company which owned a number of gas and electric utilities throughout the eastern United States.

When Geist bought the Cloister Inn he already owned the Seaview Golf Club in Absecon, near Atlantic City in New Jersey, which he founded in 1914. Golf had become his favorite sport. Since the early 1920s he had regularly spent the winter season in Palm Beach and had built a house on Golf View Road in 1923. The towered Spanish Revival-style house, designed by Marion Sims Wyeth, who later completed commissions for Geist in Boca Raton, was according to the *Palm Beach Post* "an ideal setting for entertaining," because of its interesting architecture and beautiful interiors.

One story claimed that Geist purchased the failed Mizner development to start his own club because the Everglades Club in Palm Beach denied his application for membership. According to author Theodore Pratt's recounting of the legend, a furious Geist resolved to build a club so exclusive that "members of the Everglades Club would be excluded. It would also be so magnificent that the Evergladers would look like a tarpaper shack community." Pratt claimed that only the "spirit" of the legend was true as Geist never submitted his name to the Everglades Club membership committee. As a loud, vulgar man with "uncouth manners," he knew it would reject him.

Although the Pratt details added a colorful twist to the story, neither it, nor the legend have any basis in fact. Clarence Geist became a member of the Everglades Club in the early twenties and retained his membership even after he purchased the Cloister Inn. In this period sewing machine heir Paris Singer owned the club. While Singer appointed a socially prominent and well-to-do board of governors which he consulted on membership questions and club rules, ultimately he made the final decisions. Singer, who considered Geist a friend, sponsored his membership and encouraged his purchase of a lot in the Golf View Road subdivision which the club owner developed to

The architectural rendering of the original Schultze and Weaver proposal for the Boca Raton Club shows the lakefront facade with the Mizner Cloister Inn almost completely engulfed by the massive new additions. The large Gothic window frames at the center of the addition mark the Cathedral Dining Room. The low one-story wing shown on the right was never built.

give members the privacy and convenience of living on the Everglades' grounds.

Clarence Geist, a self-made man who spent his youth on the western frontier, had great self-confidence and liked to have his way in all situations. Nonetheless, there is no evidence he was crude and vulgar. In fact, his family remembers him as polite, considerate, and always kind. Articles in Palm Beach newspapers mention the Geists as guest at various social events and list socially important individuals as their guests. Moreover, when the second most important social club, the Bath and Tennis, opened in 1927, the Geists became charter members. In reality, Geist had mentioned several years earlier his desire to establish a winter club in Florida similar to his summer club in New Jersey. As an original investor in the Mizner development he knew the Boca Raton property. He also knew that eventually it would be worth many times the price paid the bankruptcy trustees.

In announcing that he proposed to greatly expand the Cloister Inn and hire golf course planners Toomey and Flynn to completely reconstruct the hotel's two courses, Geist said he had absolute faith "in Florida and its future. As long as Florida sunshine continues to shine people will come to Florida." He also stated that like his Seaview Club, the Boca Raton facility would become a private "sportsman's paradise."

For the additions to the Cloister Inn, Geist called upon the New York architectural firm of Schultze and Weaver. The firm was already well known for its work in South Florida. In Miami alone it had completed the Biltmore Hotel in Coral Gables, the Roney Plaza Hotel in Miami Beach, and the *Miami Daily News* building on Biscayne Boulevard. All three of these buildings were modeled on the fifteenth-century Tower of Giralda in Seville, Spain. In 1925 Schultze and Weaver received the commission for a large office building in downtown Miami and another to replace the old wooden Breakers Hotel in Palm Beach that had been destroyed in a spectacular mid-season fire.

The 300-room addition planned by the architects called for a six-story building surrounding a 350-foot square entrance courtyard. While the new design incorporated the small Cloister Inn, the size of the addition almost completely engulfed the earlier structure. A palm-lined drive led from Camino Real to the entrance. A porte cochere provided a sheltered entry into the new main lobby which stretched the entire length of the northern wing of the building. Large new kitchens and laundry facilities were added at this time as well as an indoor saltwater swimming pool with both men's and women's locker rooms. The Mizner hotel enclosed the new courtyard on the east while the additions formed its other three sides. Schultze and Weaver retained Mizner's public rooms, though they added the large lakefront Cathedral Dining Room and converted Mizner's dining room into a lounge. The architects kept the large patio of the Cloister Inn and included several smaller patios in the additions. One of these, next to the Cathedral Dining Room on the lakefront, had an outdoor dance floor.

The collapse of the land boom also stopped construction on the southeastern Florida coast. The announcement of the $2 million addition to the Cloister Inn seemed an encouraging sign for economic recovery. When the Jacksonville firm of Seaboard and Southern Construction received the contract in April, newspapers called it the largest announced for the entire East Coast in 1928. The construction timetable outlined work to start in August with completion in October 1929 in time for the club to open for the 1929-1930 season.

Geist now formally founded both the Boca Raton Club and the Spanish River Land Company. The Boca Raton Syndicate, organized and managed by Geist, who subscribed $595,000 of its original $1 million capital, controlled both. Twenty-nine Syndicate members subscribed between $5,000 and $25,000. When this subscription proved inadequate for Geist's purposes, he amended the syndicate agreement in April to raise additional capital.

Geist called for additional capital to come from seven hundred members of the club who would pay $5,000 for their membership and in return receive fifty shares of stock in the Spanish River Land Company. He planned to raise a total of $3,500,000 of which approximately $1,000,000 would pay the initial cost of the club property with the balance used for additions and "betterments" to the clubhouse. For the $1,000,000 the club received title to the Cloister Inn with its Mizner Industry furnishings, and the land for

two golf courses and a bathing beach on the Atlantic Ocean. The Spanish River Land Company retained ownership of all other property acquired by Geist in the bankruptcy sale.

In the *Propsectus* for the Boca Raton Club its owners promised every facility for outdoor life and sports. According to this brochure, one eighteen-hole golf course designed by Toomey and Flynn and a nine-hole "practice" course was completed with a second eighteen-hole course under construction. A new deepwater inlet with jetty gave immediate assess to the "best" deep-sea fishing off the Florida coast. Captain Burham Knight, "one of the most expert and reliable fishing guides" in the state planned to move his fleet to the club the next season. A bathing beach with cabanas was promised for an oceanfront location. Tennis courts were under construction, trap shooting and riding were provided, and a "Healthatorium" for ladies and one for men allowed for sun baths. Moreover, the East Coast Canal passed within a few hundred feet of the Boca Raton Club docks, allowing members to arrive by private yacht.

For the convenience of its members the club also supplied a children's dining room, separate dining rooms for maids and chauffeurs, a garage for two hundred cars, a barber shop and "beauty parlor," and a number of shops including a cigar and newsstand, jewelry shop, men and women's clothing stores, a drugstore, and a brokers' office. The club also promised to maintain the luxury of the old Mizner inn,

The Seaboard and Southern Construction Company of Jacksonville began construction of the Schultze-and-Weaver-designed additions to the small Cloister Inn in late 1928. The original $2,000,000 contract raised hopes on the Gold Coast that the real estate boom of the 1920s might be revived. Although Geist ultimately spent $3,500,000 in completing his new club, the real estate market remained stagnate in Boca Raton and in most of the southeastern section of Florida until after World War II.

announcing that the Palm Beach and New York "art dealer," Ohan S. Berberyan, assisted by Charles of London and Paul Chalfin, James Deering's decorator at Vizcaya, were in charge of furnishing the club. After the payment of the $5,000 membership fee, which gave each member a proprietary interest in the club, dues for all this luxury were a modest $100 a year.

Although some club members checked in before Christmas, the arrival of Clarence Geist on January 5, 1930, marked the opening of the new Boca Raton Club. Geist, his daughter Elizabeth, and young nephew Bradley Geist came to Palm Beach in the financier's private railroad car and then drove to the club. In later years Geist's annual arrival at the Florida East Coast

Railway depot in Boca Raton was marked by the attendance of the staff of the club, the citizens of the town, and the hotel orchestra. Although Geist paid for the construction of a new and more elegant depot for Boca Raton, the facilities remained incomplete until May 1930.

For the next eight years, Geist ran the Boca Raton Club much as Paris Singer had the Everglades Club in the early 1920s. While its members might have a proprietary interest in the club, Geist controlled over 50 percent of the shares. Geist insisted the club remain completely private. Only members and their announced guests could gain admission through the guarded gates. While other private clubs regularly

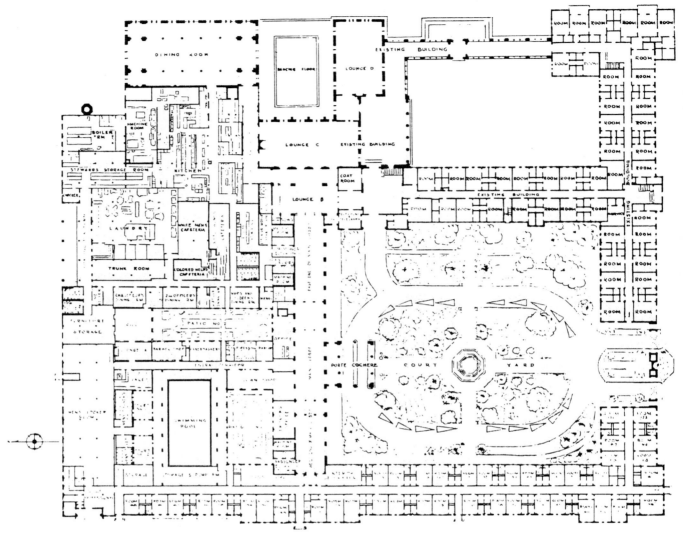

Ground Plan, Boca Raton Club House

Schultze and Weaver carefully integrated the Mizner-designed Cloister Inn, seen at the top right of the floor plan, into the new Boca Raton Club. The many patios and courtyards also carried out Mizner's ideas for adapting Florida buildings to the state's climate. When the new Boca Raton Club opened for the 1929-1930 season its facilities offered every luxury requested by its demanding members.

invited reporters to write about their important members and helped them fill society columns with stories of dinners and balls, the Boca Raton Club never made the names of its members or guests public and never gave publicity to its social functions. While all seven hundred members were well known in American social and financial life, one source said that almost none of the tourists who could see its pink towers as they drove down Federal Highway had ever heard of the Boca Raton Club.

C. O. Smith of the Southam newspaper chain was one of the few reporters ever to visit the club and to interview Geist. Even Smith revealed no members' names and while saying the clubhouse was an exquisite home in the Spanish style built to accommodate several hundred members, he failed to describe it, saying his

The buildings of the town of Boca Raton seem very far away in this photograph taken from the roof of the Boca Raton Club during the construction of the Schultze-and-Weaver-designed additions. The hollow-tile and stucco walls and red-tile roofs blended well with the original Cloister Inn section of the club.

article was to brief to do justice to its beauty. In fact, most of the article told of Clarence Geist's accomplishments from his days as a horse trader to his ownership of two of America's most exclusive private clubs. When asked how he built his fortune, Geist replied: "Hard work, some luck and a watchful eye open for the right opportunity, explain most fortunes. Opportunities usually do not come with bells and whistles. You have to discover them without signals." While Geist went into land speculation and utilities to make money, he said he was never concerned about the clubs paying their way. They were the hobby of a man whose fortune was assured.

Almost the only other source for the Geist years at the Boca Raton Club is Theodore Pratt. In a *Saturday Evening Post* article and later in *The Story of Boca Raton*, Pratt told of the eccentric multimillionaire who ran his club like the lord of a medieval fiefdom. The Geist who marched through the club lobby in his long johns and bathrobe, who upon entering an elevator ordered its operator to take him to the sixth floor "with the rest of the social register occupants getting off on the way down," who held the weekly movie until his arrival and then imperiously announced "I'm here" to the projectionist, or who ordered his chauffeur to follow him across the golf course in case he became tired and wished to ride. Some of these tales illustrate bad manners, some bad taste, while most just

seem very unlikely. Would the man who had a passionate love of golf, who had developed and owned two golf clubs, and who spent hundreds of thousands of dollars to build and maintain them risk their destruction by ordering his driver to follow him "straight down the fairways and up the greens?"

Pratt also relates that Geist came to fear kidnapping, saying he constantly changed the location of his rooms in the club, hired 24-hour bodyguards and a police dog for protection, refused to have his photograph taken, and kept over a million dollars in his checking account to pay ransom. At the same time, Pratt quoted a Palm Beacher as saying anyone who knew Geist realized that a kidnapper might soon regret his action. Again, while many wealthy Americans feared kidnapping after the Lindbergh case, Pratt's story seems greatly exaggerated.

The major difference between Paris Singer in Palm Beach and Clarence Geist in Boca Raton relates to the size of their respective communities and the wealth of their citizens. Palm Beach was not only larger, its well-to-do residents could afford to build the Bath and Tennis Club when they believed Singer's management of the Everglades had become too dictatorial. In tiny Boca Raton most of the residents were dependent on Geist and his club for their jobs, and realized that the Spanish River Land Company owned over half of all the property in the town. During the 1930s, Geist's power over the little community became almost complete.

During the summer of 1929 construction of the Schultze and Weaver additions to the Boca Raton Club had reached the roof over the six-story-high northern wing. Here workmen are installing the ornate finales to the stylized battlements which give the building its Venetian flair.

Shortly after Geist purchased the Cloister Inn he had his agents approached the Town Commission about building a new water purification and softening plant. At the time the town owed a large debt for the many improvements, such as the new Town Hall, made during the boom period. It also was unable to meet the payments due the American-LaFrance Company for Old Betsy, the town's first fire engine. Nonetheless, at a June 13, 1928 meeting the commission voted unanimously to put the water plant issue before the voters after the completion of plans and specifications.

On June 16, 1928, the commission voted to hire the J. B. McCrary Engineering Corporation, designers of the Cocoa, Florida system, which the commission said it had "investigated thoroughly," to plan a Boca Raton plant. It then passed an emergency ordinance, based on public health and safety, to construct the new waterworks. The commission included a provision to borrow $55,000 and to issue bonds, at 6 percent interest, "to the person or corporation loaning the same." By saying a grave emergency existed, the ordinance could take effect immediately.

Clarence Geist later mentioned that he took great pride in loaning the money to build the waterworks. He said:

"Water is the foundation of every community, and without GOOD water, no one will ever come into this town. . . . In going through any town, if you will notice the houses that have been sprayed at the time of watering the flowers and lawn, if the water is bad

water it will color the house brown, if the water is good water it will not effect the houses, and the same applies to the kidneys and stomach. There are three things that kill people—The first is bad water, the second is bad whisky, and the third good whisky." Like his medieval counterpart, the lord of Boca Raton wished to protect the health and morals of his subjects.

Geist's loan bought one of the most modern waterwork plants in the state of Florida. Its lime-softening system served the town until the 1960s when it no longer could produce the quantity of water that Boca Raton's growing population demanded. Bill Prendergast, director of Boca Raton's public works in the 1950s, later recalled that when a part in the old system needed replacement the surprised Chicago manufacturer sent a representative to look at the equipment as its records no longer extended back into the 1920s and it knew nothing of that model.

In a talk given in the late 1920s Geist called upon the citizens of Boca Raton to give up politics. He said that a politician never had any idea of helping anyone except himself and that the town could be saved from the problems produced by politics by paying a salary to only the town clerk, the superintendent of the waterworks, and the policeman. As Geist owned most of the property in the town he wanted to see taxes as low as possible. While calling for cooperation, "the people living in this town (should) get together and talk things over, just like a City of Brotherly Love,"

Guards manned the gates of the gigantic entrance courtyard of the Boca Raton Club twenty-four hours a day. Only members, or their invited guests gained admittance to the lushly landscaped grounds of the tropical "millionaire's club." Several sources mentioned that Clarence Geist hired a French landscape architect to give the courtyard and the other areas of the club's huge expanse of grounds their special appeal.

Geist proposed to insure his control of the town government by calling for a new charter.

The Florida legislature responded in the spring of 1929 by approving a new charter. This in turn was ratified by a May referendum of the Boca Raton voters who also passed a bill authorizing the town government to settle and adjust all taxes due up to 1928. After abolishing the three-person commission made up of mayor, clerk, and constable, the new charter called for a government consisting of elected mayor, clerk, and five-member council. These officers stood for election in July 1929 for terms running until the last day in February 1931.

The July election neither ended politics, nor produced the harmony of Geist's "City of Brotherly Love." A report from the *Palm Beach Times* told of a "street altercation" between the old mayor, John G. Brown, and commissioner Leo C. Godwin, a candidate for the new council. Police Chief I. L. Blackman called

the argument and "fracas" personal and political in nature. It ended when Blackman disarmed the mayor who "brandished a gun." Brown, who had been elected Boca Raton's first mayor in 1924, objected to Geist's demand to change the date of elections. As the majority of the town's citizens agreed with Geist, this ended Brown's political career. Fred C. Aiken, one of the owners of the tract of land west of town with the twenty-nine Mizner-designed houses, won election as mayor over Tony Brenk; Beulah Butler beat out Louise Brenk to remain clerk; and Harry Chesebro, J. C. Mitchell, E. J. Bender, Leo C. Godwin, and W. C. Young composed the new council.

The new charter set a February date for all succeeding elections. This meant that the club, with its limited December to May season, would be open during the town elections. According to Pratt, old-time Boca Raton citizens swore that Geist insisted his club employees vote to insure his control of town

The porte-cochere served as the main entrance to the Boca Raton Club. The French doors to the left also led to the main lobby stretching the full length of this wing of the clubhouse. The six-floor balconies mark some of the club's luxury suites. The ornate battlements and cornice reflected the lakeside location of the club which reminded the architects of Venice.

government and town taxes. One story claimed that "foreign chefs who were not American citizens and could barely speak English voted regularly." Although these stories may be true, at the same time, few Boca Raton citizens or their elected representatives even considered opposing the will of the town's most influential property owner.

The construction of Boca Raton's first airport shows the close relationship that developed between club and town officials. Early in 1935 Gordon B. Anderson, the club manager, told the town that many of its members now owned airplanes and wished a convenient airport and hanger facility. The town clerk made the airport a top priority and over the next two years wrote numerous letters, reports, and applications to officials of both the state and federal government to seek funds for the Boca Raton project. Neither Boca Raton nor the state had funds to build the airport. Nonetheless, the town received land considered worthless for agricultural purposes because "it was too far west" from the Model Land Company (which held the land grants given to Henry M. Flagler to build the Florida East Coast Railway) and used this land, the promise of a salary for an airport superintendent, and some labor and equipment as the basis to apply for a New Deal WPA project in 1936.

When the WPA considered the Boca Raton contribution too low, Anderson pressured the town government to increase its commitment. Ultimately Boca Raton pledged a $15,000 donation consisting of rock to pave the runways, equipment rentals, and skilled labor. When this still failed to convince the WPA, Anderson spent what he called "a very profitable day in Washington" in mid-October 1936 and work on the airport began before the end of the year. Nonetheless, lack of money ended up suspending the project before completion. When this happened Anderson arranged for the club to pay for the finishing touches and even used some club personnel to complete the job. He told town officials that waiting for a new WPA project might take months, and certainly would cost "thousands of dollars" more than doing it themselves.

Anderson wanted the airfield opened for the 1937-1938 season. The cooperation between town and club meant completion of the job in July. Although before it could be used it had to pass a federal inspection. Anderson wrote to town officials to stress to the inspectors the necessity of the Boca Raton field. The New Deal believed WPA money should be used to help the unemployed and in general stimulate depressed segments of the national economy. Anderson feared that should the airport's connection with the

The impressive new two-story lobby of the Boca Raton Club extended the entire length of the northern wing of the building. Schultze and Weaver, the architects for the additions, planned the lobby as a monumental entry to the luxurious clubhouse. It joined the old Cloister Inn section of the building and its public rooms to the new bedroom wing of the addition.

The Cloister Inn's ballroom became a lounge in the Boca Raton Club. This room, with its gigantic cypress beams, overlooked both the dance patio and Lake Boca Raton. Although most of the comfortable chairs and sofas are new, the "Papa Mizner" chair in the foreground was made by Mizner Industries for the Cloister Inn.

The entrance to the new Boca Raton Club lounge, formerly the dining room in the old Mizner Cloister Inn, was at the east end of the main lobby. The large staff of gardeners and groundskeepers also worked to produce hundreds of potted plants and flowers to decorate the public rooms of the club.

89

The Schultze-and-Weaver-designed additions for Clarence Geist to the small Cloister Inn included the Cathedral Dining Room. This lofty lakefront room provided a grand setting for the Boca Raton Club's most elegant dinners. The decoration included gold leaf columns, polychromed coffered ceiling, and gigantic Venetian chandeliers. The raised "aisle" on the right allowed the lucky diners a lake view through a series of Gothic-arched windows.

millionaire's club become known its final approval might be delayed and further projects, such as a hanger, canceled. He warned town officials to "drive home" the fact that hundreds of military planes passed over southeastern Florida and that Eastern Air Lines had no place to land between Miami and West Palm Beach. Without the field, forced landings would result in crashes as the beach sand was too soft to support a plane and sand traps and bunkers crowded area golf courses. Finally, he told the town officials "not to create the impression" that the airport was only for the convenience of the Boca Raton Club.

The correspondence between Anderson and town officials reveals both the close relationship and the obvious fact that the club was prepared to direct the town's action and even spend the town's tax money for projects it felt important. Most Boca Raton citizens accepted this relationship, believing it was also in their best interest.

As early as 1930, Geist decided to revive the faded real estate market in Boca Raton. His Spanish River Land Company commissioned Marion Sims Wyeth, the architect of his Palm Beach villa, to design two houses on Camino Real across from the club's golf course. Wyeth was one of the society architects who in the 1920s created the architectural style for Palm Beach. He came to Florida from New York City in 1919 to design the first section of Good Samaritan Hospital in West Palm Beach. A 1910 graduate of Princeton, he spent four years at the Ecole des Beaux Arts in Paris studying architecture. After an apprenticeship with Bertram Grovenor Goodhue and Carrere and Hastings (the designers of Henry M. Flagler's Palm Beach mansion), Wyeth served as a first lieutenant in the Army Air Corps during World War I. Following the war he formed a partnership in New York with Frederick Rhinelander King, a fellow Ecole des Beaux Arts student.

Wyeth had designed several other houses on Golf View Road in addition to the one for Geist. Almost across the street from the Geist villa he completed a house for the E. F. Huttons. When the Huttons decided

The Mizner-designed dining room for the Cloister Inn became the new club's main lounge. Mizner took his model for the room from a fifteenth-century hospital in Vich in Catalonia. The five arched bays supported the ceiling of beams and sapling poles. New decoration by Ohan S. Berberyan of Palm Beach and New York included large chandeliers, deep-pile rugs covering the red-waxed tile floors, and comfortable overstuffed chairs and sofas.

build a large new mansion on the island, they chose Wyeth as their architect. The result was Mar-a-Lago, the resort's most extravagant house. Before completion of the plans, Mrs. Hutton (Marjorie Merriweather Post) asked Joseph Urban, a New York City architect and set designer for the Metropolitan Opera and Flo Ziegfeld, to add the decorative details to the mansion. Although Wyeth's floor plans and general configuration of the house were retained and he remained as the associate architect, he later said of Mar-a-Lago, "It isn't my taste. It's entirely the taste of Joe Urban. I don't want anyone to think I was the architect in charge."

Wyeth designed his largest Palm Beach house for the James Donahues (she was Jesse Woolworth). On South Ocean Boulevard just north of Mar-a-Lago, the Donahue villa was later divided into five different houses and Kings Road was built through the former living room.

After the completion of the Schultze and Weaver additions to the Boca Raton Club Geist asked Wyeth to undertake several minor remodeling commissions. The two Camino Real houses, both in the typical restrained Spanish style for which Wyeth had become known in Palm Beach, were Geist's attempt to stimulate the real estate market. Shortly after the houses were finished, Frederick B. Rentschler, founder of United Aircraft Corporation and a club member, did purchase the western house. The eastern house became an annex to the club, rented to members and guests who wished to take a house for the season.

In the mid-thirties Geist decided to develop the area south of the inlet between the ocean and Intracoastal Waterway. Mizner, who called this area the Distrito de Boca Raton, believed its location and many waterfront lots made it the most desirable of all the town's subdivisions. His company limited "the privilege of purchase to those enjoying recognized social positions," and placed design and cost restrictions on the houses built in the subdivision. Although Mizner completed plans for at least eight large houses, the boom bubble burst before any could be built. Geist financed a bridge across the Intracoastal Waterway which linked this area closely to the club.

91

In 1935 Geist called upon Maurice Fatio, the partner in charge of the Palm Beach office of Treanor and Fatio, to design four houses for the area. Fatio, who had been born into a wealthy old banking family of Italian-French-Swiss ancestry on March 18, 1897, in Geneva, had come to the United States in 1920 after his graduation from Zurich's renowned Polytech. His excellent training and first-rate talent, combined with great charm, good looks, and sociable nature, soon allowed him to succeed the ailing Addison Mizner as Palm Beach's most fashionable society architect. By 1935 his clients included some of the most prominent individuals in America such as Joseph E. Widener, Otto Kahn, Harrison Williams, and Harold S. Vanderbilt and his sister Mme. Louis Jacques Balsam, the former Duchess of Marlborough.

Fatio designed all four houses in the tropical Georgian style which had become fashionable in Palm Beach. All were either three- or four-bedroom residences with numerous baths and powder rooms, extensive porches and terraces, and quarters for two or three staff. The house designed for a lot on the waterway had a natural red-brick exterior, red barrel-tile roofs, a gallery on the second floor, and white trim and shutters. The two Cocoanut Road houses were also brick and frame construction, although painted white. The fourth house, on Banyan Road, was stucco with white quoins and a second floor gallery. By placing the four houses in four different areas of the tract, Geist hoped to encourage sales of lots and promote additional construction.

Although three of the houses soon sold after their construction, they never stimulated the hoped-for

The Schultze and Weaver plans for the Boca Raton Club addition included many small patios. This lakefront patio, placed just south of the Cathedral Dining Room and north of the Cloister Inn lounge became the setting for the club's elegant afternoon tea dances. On warm nights during the season its starlighted dance floor provided romantic after-dinner entertainment. A later remodeling enclosed and roofed the patio, creating a new entrance to the Cathedral Dining Room.

...oom. Only one other house was built in the 1930s in ...is section. In 1936 James H. Howe of St. Louis, ...under of the Lewis-Howe Company, the makers of ...ms, asked Marion Sims Wyeth to design a house for ...s Camino Real lot overlooking the lake and inlet. The ...owe mansion was also designed in tropical Georgian ...yle with open galleries, porches, and numerous ...uttered French doors. Unlike the speculative houses ...esigned for Geist, the Howe house was specifically ...anned for a well-to-do client who could afford the ...xcellent detailing typical of Wyeth's Palm Beach ...ommissions.

Clarence Geist was responsible for one other Boca ...aton house built in this period. In 1937 he ...ommissioned Palm Beach architect Gustav Maass to ...esign a small house for R. F. "Red" Lawrence, the head ...reenskeeper at the Club. Maass, a graduate of the

University of Pennsylvania, had come to Florida during the land boom to join the West Palm Beach architectural firm of Harvey and Clarke. When that firm failed at the end of the boom he formed a partnership with young John L. Volk which lasted until 1935. The Lawrence house was one of several Maass designed for Boca Raton in the late 1930s. The two-story wooden house stood on extensive grounds just north of Palmetto Park Road on the west side of the Intracoastal Waterway.

Although the town's largest landowner in 1930, Clarence Geist soon met competition for that title. For one farmer, with a good amount of capital to invest, the land bust proved the making of an empire. August H. Butts, born in Lake County in Central Florida in 1884, came to Fort Lauderdale shortly after the turn of the century. By 1909 he was farming in the area and had

This aerial photograph of the early 1930s shows the additions to the Boca Raton Club stretching along the western shore of the newly dredged and channeled Lake Boca Raton. Mizner's magnificent Camino Real, lined with royal palms, marks the southern bounds of the Toomey and Flynn championship golf course. The outdoor swimming pool complex was to the left of the traffic circle marking the entrance to the club driveway. The two estates in the lower right side of the photograph were designed by Marion Sims Wyeth, the architect of Geist's Palm Beach villa, for his Spanish River Land Company. Before the completion of the two houses, Frederick B. Rentschler, the founder of United Aircraft Corporation, purchased the westernmost house. It has remained in his family's hands since.

married Natalie Swanson of Mount Dora. In the last years of the 1920s he realized that the bust in the real estate market made it possible to purchase high, well-drained farmlands west of Boca Raton at bargain prices and in some cases by only paying the taxes when former owners defaulted.

By 1933 when his son Harold graduated from the University of Florida and joined him in the business he already owned two 640-acre sections. The land proved well suited for the growth of green beans, which became the Butts Farms' specialty. In fact, Butts Farms' beans gained the reputation of being Florida's finest and they commanded a 25-cent-a-bushel premium on northern markets.

Throughout the 1930s the Butts family continued to purchase land. A second son, Clarence, was placed in charge of the irrigation system. Jeannette Butts, the eldest daughter, married Marshall DeWitt, a Delray Beach farmer, who supervised packing and shipping operations. Near the end of the decade Myrtle Butts, the youngest daughter, married Thomas Farrar Fleming, Jr., the son of a Fort Lauderdale attorney. Fleming handled financial and real estate concerns for the growing family business.

By building the best in irrigation systems and using the most up-to-date farming methods, the Butts Farms became one of the largest bean producers in Florida. In 1940 the farms regularly employed four hundred workers and added an additional five hundred migrant pickers for harvests. In that year they shipped 134,000 hampers, or three hundred boxcar loads, from their own loading docks, to the northern markets. According to *Boca Raton News* reporter Skip Sheffield, the farm contained a small village of houses for its employees, its own machine shop, office building, ice plant, and railroad shipping platform.

At its peak, the Butts farms covered thirty-five hundred acres, or around six square miles, in the Boca Raton area. Nonetheless, never more than sixteen hundred acres were under production. Harold Butts later said they purchased the additional land to keep other farmers from coming into the market and for the water. Pumps brought water to the cultivated fields from everywhere on the farm. The system was so efficient that the farm could sell surplus water to other farmers.

While the Butts family developed its farmland, the Chicago owners of the tract on the west side of town recovered from the Mizner bankruptcy, struggled to complete the twenty-nine houses and see the subdivision's streets opened and paved. Of the original owners, Hermann V. von Holst and Fred C. Aiken actually came to Florida to care for their investment. Von Holst, an architect, filed a new plat plan with the town and renamed the tract "Floresta." He derived the new east-west street names from plants and flowers, such as Alamanda, Hibiscus, and Oleander; the two north-south streets were named Cardinal and Paloma.

Von Holst took charge of completing the unfinished houses. The owners planned to rent the unoccupied ones to seasonal visitors. Von Holst also built a number of garages at the various houses. At one point, this

When Clarence Geist purchased the Cloister Inn there was no railroad passenger station in Boca Raton. Florida East Coast Railway passengers either left their trains in Delray Beach or Deerfield Beach, or alighted on the rickety wooden cargo platform at Palmetto Park Road. Geist insisted on a depot worthy of his club, and also one much closer. Chester G. Henninger, an architect for the Florida East Coast Railway, designed the new Spanish-style passenger and freight station in 1929. One story claims that Geist then purchased $200,000 of stock in the railway company to finance the station's construction. The new depot was completed for the 1930-1931 season.

activity prompted the town clerk to remind him that he had failed to secure a building permit.

Although born in Germany in 1874, as a young man von Holst came to the United States when his father, a great scholar of the Constitution, received appointment in 1891 as the first professor of history at the newly established University of Chicago. After graduating from the University of Chicago, he enrolled in the architecture program at the Massachusetts Institute of Technology. In 1904 he established his practice in Chicago and also began to teach architectural design at the Art Institute. When Frank Lloyd Wright closed his office to prepare his drawings for publication in Germany, von Holst took over Wright's commissions in progress. Although best known for his industrial work, he specialized in the construction of power plants for the Public Service Company of Northern Illinois and the Commonwealth Edison Company. He later published a book entitled *Country and Suburban*

Homes of the Prairie School Period which used many of his own innovative designs.

Von Holst moved permanently to his two-story house on Alamanda Street in 1932. In Boca Raton he served as councilman from 1934 to 1947 and again in 1948 to 1949. He became chairman of the town planning board in 1940 and served until 1953 when he was made an honorary life member.

Fred C. Aiken also came to Boca Raton to personally manage his Floresta property. A native of LaCrosse, Wisconsin, Aiken was a pioneer in the distribution of motion pictures. One of his earliest companies had been acquired by Sears-Roebuck. He later sold a second business to the General Film Company and retired as manager of Pathe's midwestern branch when he moved to Boca Raton in 1928. Aiken was elected mayor in the July 1929 election and received re-election for the next ten years. He then served an additional ten years as city clerk.

Clarence and Florence Geist on their arrival at the Florida East Coast Railway depot to open the season at the Boca Raton Club. Most of the club staff, many town residents, and the club orchestra regularly came to the station to greet Geist's yearly arrival. One description of the utilities magnate called him rotund, a scant six-feet tall, with a jolly face, piercing gray-blue eyes and blondish thinning hair. Ann Rentscher Cassady said Florence Geist was "very attractive and had beautiful, creamy skin." Legend claims that Geist refused to allow his photograph taken because of his fear of kidnappers. Certainly few photographs of either Clarence or Florence Geist can be found.

Throughout the thirties the owners of Floresta planted trees and shrubs, saw that the streets were finally paved, and attempted to keep the houses rented during the season. Their rental brochure, showing a birds-eye view of Boca Raton drawn by von Holst, said Floresta meant "A beautiful rural place." The houses, and also lots, were for sale, and as the decade ended many new residents arrived.

The land-boom bust followed just three years later by the stock market crash, produced particularly depressed times for the citizens of southeastern Florida. Formerly prosperous residents now watched their pennies. Floy Mitchell remembered how she proudly made her own dresses with just fifty cents worth of material, and how neighbors willingly shared both a good catch after a day's fishing and their abundant garden crops. Nonetheless, the Boca Raton Club brought a means of livelihood to local residents that other citizens of the Gold Coast failed to share in those depressed times.

The widening and deepening of the East Coast Canal (now the Intracoastal Waterway) by the federal government helped stimulate an interest in yachting and motorboating on the southeastern coast of Florida. For the Boca Raton Club it allowed members to make the trip south by means of their private yachts. Theodore Pratt claimed that Clarence Geist loved to wear his four-stripe yachting coat as commodore of the Royal Boca Raton Yacht Club, though the club consisted only of the boats of members anchored at the lakeside docks.

Capt. Burham Knight, "one of the most expert and reliable fishing guides in Florida," moved his fishing boats to the Boca Raton Club in time for its first season. The Prospectus for the club told of the program of cutting a channel from Lake Boca Raton to the ocean and building a jetty on the ocean side for all-weather protection of the entrance. The new inlet allowed the fleet to reach the fishing grounds very quickly.

Boca Raton Club photographers were always ready to document the fishing abilities of members. With the best deep-sea fishing just off the Florida shore, the picture of a large sailfish and a fashionably dressed and proud victor in the battle of the deep, was often duplicated on the club's Lake Boca Raton boat landing.

The towers of both the Cloister Inn and the additions by Schultze and Weaver rise just beyond the new outdoor pool of the Boca Raton Club. Located on the lakefront, just north of Camino Real, this pool served club and later hotel guests until the late 1960s when the site was taken for the new convention center. The small corner towers of the pool pavilions were incorporated into the new building.

In the mid-thirties Geist asked Palm Beach architect Maurice Fatio to convert the little-used pool into an auditorium. As the acoustics proved exceptionally good, this became a popular setting for many club entertainments. The weekly movies were later celebrated in club legend as the scene of Geist's most lordly behavior. After all the guests were seated, Geist would arrive and shout to the projectionist, "I'm here," a signal that the show could begin.

The Schultze and Weaver additions for the Boca Raton Club included a large indoor saltwater pool. One source claimed that the pool was strictly segregated by sex. Most club guests came to Florida for the sun and climate and the indoor pool soon proved unpopular.

Every possible service was available to the members of the Boca Raton Club. The fleet of limousines owned by George Pennell seems to stretch down the club entrance driveway as far as the eye can see. These cars were always ready to whisk guests to Pompano Beach for a dinner at Cap's Place, or to Palm Beach for an afternoon of shopping on Worth Avenue.

The Cabana Club provided informal dining rooms, card lounges, and a third Olympic-sized pool for the Boca Raton Club complex. Over the years its lavish luncheon buffet attracted members and guests daily. The Cabana Club also included two hundred private cabanas on two levels in a semicircle facing the ocean. Each had a sun deck furnished with chaise lounges and chairs and partially covered by an awning, a bar, and two dressing rooms with connecting shower. Sunbathing decks, strictly separated by sex, were located above the second level of cabanas. Members could rent cabanas by the season or during their stay at the club. For guests without cabanas there were locker rooms, and deck chairs and colorful umbrellas on the immaculately kept beach.

In his memoir Reminiscences of a Pioneer, Harley Gates said that local residents founded the Boca Raton Hunt Club in January 1927. Its original sixty members had twenty good saddle horses at their disposal. Clint Moore, a paving contractor from Tennessee, supplied many of the mounts. Geist recognized the interest and continued to provide facilities so that club members and guests might also ride.

Tennis awards for junior girls at the Boca Raton Club brought out fathers and teacher. From left to right, "Babe" Dooley, granddaughter of James Howe, maker of Tums; Gordon B. Anderson, general manager of the club; two unidentified girls; Frederick Rentschler, chairman of United Aircraft Corporation; Val Yavorsky, the club tennis pro; Peggy Anderson; and Ann Rentschler (Cassady). During the 1930s the club tennis courts were located just south of the old Cloister Inn and north of the outdoor swimming pool.

Mizner had reserved a section of the Boca Raton beach for the guests of the Cloister Inn. Here he built colorful canvas and frame cabanas "reminiscent of the Lido," where guests, "garbed in the gay Lido pajamas," were served lunch and "dainty" sandwiches. Geist's first Syndicate agreement also mentioned "a suitable bathing beach on the Atlantic Ocean." Construction on the Cabana Club began in December 1930. The porte-cochere, its Spanish architecture echoing that of the main clubhouse, provided entrance to the large semi-circular two-story structure. When the Cabana Club was razed in 1980 to become the site of the Addison condominiums, the porte-cochere was saved and moved to the county beach at the end of Camino Real on the ocean.

A very dapper Mayor John G. Brown poses on a visit to the Cloister Inn. Brown, who became mayor when the town of Boca Raton was incorporated in 1924, served until Geist requested changes in the charter in 1929. He was succeeded by Fred Aiken of Floresta. During the July 1929 election a "street altercation" between Mayor Brown and Commissioner Leo G. Godwin ended when the police chief disarmed the mayor.

This photograph, perhaps made at the dedication of the Boca Raton Town Hall, shows a selection of leading citizens of the 1920s. Lillian Race Williams is in the foreground. In the front row, from the left, are Eula Raulerson, Ruby Bender, Clementine Brown, town clerk Beulah Butler, Mary Alice Lamont, Erma Habercorn, Pauline Raulerson, Mayor John Brown, George Akins (who was later the town clerk), and B. B. Raulerson. In the rear row, from the left, are Mrs. C. W. Stokes, longtime postmistress Peg Young, Florence Purdom, Audrey Purdom, Mamie Riley, John Cramer (who constructed the building), Mamie Habercorn, Mrs. Bill Sherman, Mrs. George Young, Lorene Cramer, and Annie Raulerson.

Boca Raton motorcycle policeman Eugene Carter stands with club groundskeeper Clyde Miller on the road running through the golf course to the west of the main clubhouse. This April 1932 photograph shows the completed Schultze and Weaver additions to the building and the maturing of the 1929-1930 landscaping and golf course paintings.

Although the town of Boca Raton was deeply in debt in 1928, after tax payers voted overwhelmingly in favor, the commission passed an emergency ordinance to build a new pumping station and water treatment plant. Clarence Geist took great pride in loaning the $55,000 at low interest that built the new system which with only minor additions and adjustments served the town until the 1960s.

Clarence Geist financed a new water treatment plant for Boca Raton in 1928. Sometimes nicknamed "Waterboy," Geist owned a number of utilities companies which supplied water to suburban Philadelphia communities. He personally campaigned for a pure water system for his new club and backed the construction of the new facility which at the time was one of the most modern in Florida.

The Boca Raton School was built in the early twenties. Until 1937 the stucco walls contrasted with white pilasters, door arches, and window frames. In that year a new auditorium was added and the appearance of the old building modernized with a new color scheme. Students could attend the Boca Raton School through the eighth grade. Boca Raton students traveled to Delray Beach for high school classes until the 1960s.

This Boca Raton School photograph, probably from the early 1920s, shows the students of teacher Clementine Brown, wife of John Brown, who became Boca Raton's first mayor. The children's names read like a roster of local pioneers. In the front row, from the left, are Pauline Raulerson, Dixie Sellers, Ivy Raulerson, Theron Dillon, Grace Boresman with Carl Douglas in front, three unidentified students, Paul Sellers, and Junior Raulerson. In the back row are Myrtle Lee Raulerson, Odas Tanner, Clifford Purdom, unidentified, and Elizabeth Dillon. Clementine Brown retired from teaching in the mid-1920s to have a family. With the Depression she returned to the profession to help support her children, although her husband's quarrel with Clarence Geist prevented her from teaching at the Boca Raton School again.

In this school photograph taken a few years later many of the same students can be identified. From the left in the front row are Robert Jourgan, Pauline Williams, Grace Douglas, Pauline Raulerson, Ivy Raulerson, Grace Boresman, Dara Burns, Odas Tanner, and Clifford Purdom in front. In the second row are Vinton Long, Robert Burns, the teacher Alice Presley, Myrtle Lee Raulerson, Minnie Burns, Lulu Burns, and Ernestine Purdom.

A Boca Raton School photograph taken in a still later year pictures a third teacher identified only as Theodora. Most of the children in the earlier photos have moved on to high school in Delray Beach or left the area. Bernice Dean and Jackie Blackman are on the immediate left of the teacher while in the middle row Junior Raulerson is the first person on the left, Buddy Gates the third, and Iris Blackman the fourth. Carl Douglas is the first person in the top row. The little boy to the right of the teacher was probably from the Japanese settlement of Yamato.

Although later called the Geist house, this red brick and tile-roof house was one of four built by the Spanish River Land Company in the mid-1930s to stimulate the Boca Raton real estate market. Designed by fashionable Palm Beach architect Maurice Fatio, this house stretched along the Intracoastal Waterway in what today is known as the estates section. The most elegantly detailed of the four houses, it contained an airy cypress-paneled living room and formal dining room as well as a spacious porch with waterway views. In 1989 the owner of the house decided to tear it down and build two new houses on the lot. Public protests may have saved the house, when a private developer moved it from its old location and up the Intracoastal Waterway to the northwestern section of town.

Maurice Fatio designed this Cocoanut Road house for Clarence Geist's Spanish River Land Company in 1936. The company sold it the next year to Russell McIntosh who rented it during the summers to Dr. William O'Donnell, the resident physician of the Boca Raton Club. During World War II McIntosh also leased it to various officers of the air base, including Col. Frank Fisher. The white brick house has many details often found in Palm Beach houses of the era.

Clarence Geist probably commissioned this house from Palm Beach architect Gustav Maass for his popular head greenskeeper, "Red" Lawrence, in 1937. The two-story wooden house had open decks on both floors and a large screened porch overlooking the extensively landscaped grounds and the Intracoastal Waterway. Boca Raton realtor F. Byron Parks later owned the house as did Gerald and Carter Coughlan. Gerry Coughlan was an ardent fisherman who kept his boat at his backyard dock. In 1978, after nineteen years in the house, the Coughlans sold to new owners who planned to remodel and enlarge the original structure. Then, after vandals damaged it, the new owners decided to build a new house and demolished the old one.

James H. Howe, founder of the Lewis-Howe Company, the makers of Tums, commissioned Palm Beach architect Marion Sims Wyeth to design this large tropical Georgian house for the south shore of Lake Boca Raton in 1938. The formal entry led to an open gallery overlooking a sheltered patio. To the right Wyeth placed three guest rooms, while to the rear, overlooking a lakefront terrace, he positioned the living and dining rooms, separated by a large sun porch. A gallery, on the north side of the entrance patio, provided a formal entrance to the dining room. A second floor contained the family bedrooms and staff rooms. By all accounts, this was the most lavish of all the houses built in Boca Raton in the 1930s. Although preservationists protested, the house was razed in 1973 to make way for the Bridge Hotel.

This white brick and frame house at Cocoanut Road and Via Cabana was a 1936 design by Palm Beach architect Maurice Fatio. The second-floor West Indies-style gallery shelters the formal entry to the house. The second door on the left allowed the guests to gain access to their rooms without disturbing the family. At one time Gordon B. Anderson, general manager of the Boca Raton Club for Clarence Geist, and later general manager of the Boca Raton Hotel and Club after World War II, owned this house.

In the fall of 1929, Clarence Geist commissioned aerial photography of his Boca Raton holdings. Unfortunately, the pilot crashed, although with only minor damage to his aircraft. Gordon Anderson, general manager of the Boca Raton Club, drew upon this experience in arguing the need for an airport in Boca Raton.

The sign in front of Fred and Lottie Aiken's Floresta house says Hibiscus Street. Hermann von Holst's plan for Floresta called for streets to be landscaped according to their names. Thus the Aikens planted a hibiscus hedge. Although the street remained unpaved, the new stripped awnings and trellis connecting the porch and garage show the Aikens' dedication to improving the subdivision.

August H. Butts began buying farmland to the west of Boca Raton in the last years of the 1920s. He became the area's largest landowner in the 1930s and Butts Farms' green beans gained the reputation of being Florida's finest. By the time of his death in 1955 the farm encompassed thirty-five hundred acres and was one of the largest bean farms in the state of Florida. Town Center Mall, Royal Oak Hills, Boca Raton Square, and many other western Boca Raton developments were built on the former land of Butts Farms.

Natalie Swanson Butts was born in Central Florida in 1883. She married August Butts in Mount Dora in 1906 and they came to Fort Lauderdale where he began farming. In the following years they had two sons, Harold and Clarence, and two daughters, Jeannette and Myrtle. The sons and the daughters' husbands all joined in helping to run the family's farms. Natalie Butts died at age ninety-two in 1975.

Harold Butts built this oceanfront house in 1939. One of only a few beach houses in Boca Raton, it was designed by Palm Beach architect Gustav Maass. The red brick house sat perched on the beach dune, allowing broad ocean views. Butts came to Boca Raton from Fort Lauderdale when the family purchased extensive farmlands to the west of the town in the late 1920s.

This is Hermann V. von Holst's bird's-eye view of Boca Raton in the 1930s. His brochure, promised the pleasure of awakening each day "to the song of birds," of driving quickly to the ocean beach, and of living "in the clean, sweet air" and beneficent sunshine. Although all the major town amenities such as the Boca Raton Club, Cabana Club, bathing pavilion, and depot are depicted on this map, Floresta is shown conveniently close to both downtown and the beach.

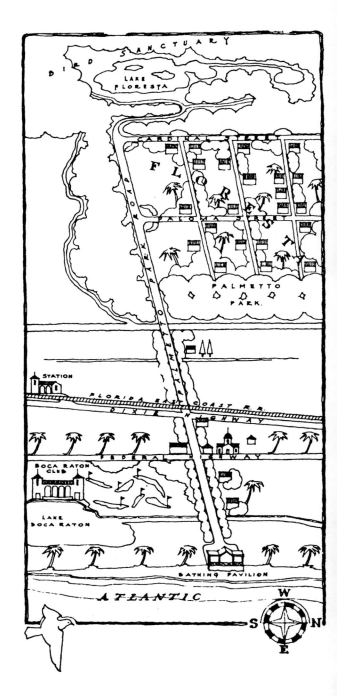

Fred Aiken was one of the Chicago investors who recovered ownership of the land west of Boca Raton with the twenty-nine Mizner-designed houses. The Chicago group had originally sold the land to Mizner in 1925. The development company's inability to make the payments ultimately forced it into bankruptcy. Aiken, who became mayor of Boca Raton in 1929 is shown examining the green beans which were Boca Raton's best-known winter agricultural crop during the 1930s and 1940s. The beans were of such quality that they sold at a premium on the northern market.

Floresta needed much work to turn it into "a delightful country place" when the former owners purchased their property through a bankruptcy sale. The Mizner Development Corporation built twenty-nine houses in this isolated western section before its failure. The new owners and their wives labored to landscape and furnish the houses and rent them to seasonal guests.

Hermann V. von Holst, a Chicago architect and large landowner in Floresta, designed the lacy pavilion at the oceanfront and Palmetto Park Road in the 1930s. Boca Raton citizens were fond of spending hot summer evenings before air conditioning visiting with friends and enjoying the cool ocean breezes. This photograph, one of the few showing the pavilion, was taken after the Boy Scouts salvaged an anchor from the ocean in 1948. A hurricane destroyed this pavilion in the 1950s.

Fred and Lottie Aiken invited a large group of family and friends for a New Years Day party in 1935. Aiken, who served as Boca Raton mayor between 1929 and 1939, is in the suit coat, to the left of the fountain sculpture. This patio is sheltered from the street by an arbor Aiken built to connect his Floresta house and garage. The attire of the guests suggests a warm beginning for 1935.

Boca Raton's first filling station was just south of Town Hall on the corner of Federal Highway and Palmetto Park Road. Clifton Harvell, on the left, the second owner, purchased the station from Guy Bender. The other men pictured are Paul Sellers and Marion "Cap" Edwards. The latticework building between the station and Town Hall was the repair garage.

The Boca Raton Girl Scout Troop is on an outing to the seaside pavilion at the end of Palmetto Park Road. The scout leader on the left is Jeannette DeWitt, a daughter of August and Natalie Butts.

One of Boca Raton's best-known residents during the 1930s was Lillian Race Williams. In 1918 her parents bought the Myrick house which remained her home until 1976. During these years she loved cars and had several, including this roadster. She was a familiar sight around town in her car, a favorite dog's head often hanging out the window.

This photograph from the Boca Raton Historical Society files is labeled "Mrs. Peyton and daughters Edith and Ethel in Por la Mar." The Por la Mar subdivision on the east side of the Intracoastal Waterway and just south of Palmetto Park Road, remained separate from Clarence Geist's Spanish River Land Company holdings in the 1930s.

In his memoirs of early days in Boca Raton, Max Hutkin recalled arriving in town in 1936 to take over a little grocery store on Dixie Highway. While he and his wife Nettie expected to stay in a small cottage with his Uncle Harry Brown's family, instead they found the Browns serving as summer caretakers for the town's most impressive oceanfront mansion and that their spacious room received a cooling ocean breeze. Dr. E. Stanley Robbins built the modified Prairie-style house sometime in the late teens or early twenties. Although severely damaged in the 1928 hurricane, in 1932 Dr. Robbins sold the house of W. J. Southam, a Canadian publisher. Its many broad windows and extensive terraces adapted well to service as Hermansson's Restaurant and in later years as the Ocean View Restaurant. By 1963 beach residents complained that owner H. Busch Hodde had allowed the stately landmark to deteriorate. After the fire department called it a hazard, the house, located just south of Palmetto Park Road, was demolished in August 1964.

During the 1930s there were only a few houses on the Boca Raton beach. This shingled bungalow, owned by J. E. Nelson, was one of three originally located just north of Palmetto Park Road. The other two houses burned in July 1927, while the Nelson house became Smitty's Driftwood Restaurant.

In December 1939 the Boca Raton Club Board of Directors proposed to restructure its millions of dollars in debts. The C. H. Geist Trust agreed to accept new bonds that covered only 16 percent of the debt owed by the club and the Spanish River Land Company so that "Boca Raton may continue in the future." To support the lowered debt the club proposed a "more liberal" membership plan, thus increasing its income.

C H A P T E R   IV

THE WAR YEARS

Throughout the 1930s Clarence Geist attempted to develop the holdings of the Spanish River Land Company by constructing houses and placing building lots on the market. He encouraged members and potential members of the Boca Raton Club to build winter residences in the town. Nonetheless, he never promoted the large-scale type of land sales of the earlier boom period. Writer Theodore Pratt suggested that Geist never wished Boca Raton to grow too large because he liked the idea of the club dominating the town, and of his domination of the club. When Geist died in June 1938, it was discovered that neither the land company nor the club had ever made a profit. In fact, Geist had subsidized the club's operation every year since its founding. While his death could have meant a disaster for the town of Boca Raton, Geist had foreseen the problems and created the C. H. Geist Trust to allow the club to continue.

According to Ann Rentschler Cassady, Florence Geist continued operating the club in much the same manner as her late husband. A 1941 article from the *Palm Beach Daily News* also suggested there were few changes under her management. It told of the stay of Archduke Otto, pretender to the throne of the Austro-Hungarian Empire, at the "snorty Boca Raton Club where he's as safe from autograph hunters as a hermit at the North Pole." The writer goes on to say that the visitor must pass first through a gate marked "private," and then after a drive up a beautifully landscaped road comes to a second gate. Here "about a half dozen guards . . . jump out in front of the car like a defending army." If the visitor has the "proper credentials" admission is gained to the "super-luxury hotel-like club," where "an eminently correct sense of gloom pervades all."

An article in a Chicago newspaper the following year, while calling the club one of the most beautiful in America, said Boca Raton had only a five hundred person permanent population and supported only two general stores, two service stations, a restaurant, and a tavern. The article also said that wealthy Chicagoans who usually spend the winter at the club would now need to look elsewhere as the Army had taken over the entire resort. Drollene Brown, in "World War II in Boca Raton: The Home Front," *The Spanish River Papers*, told of Mayor J. C. Mitchell's trip to Washington, D.C., to convince government officials that the little Gold Coast town would make a perfect Army base. Mitchell found Washington crowded with mayors from little towns and cities across the nation still reeling from the effects of the long depression and all positive that they had the right site for a base. Shuffled from the War Department to the Navy and to the Army Air Corps, Mitchell finally received a promise that Boca Raton would at least be considered as an air base site.

The Army Air Corps had already decided it needed a base in Southeast Florida. When the United States entered World War II, radar was relatively new and its uses as a tool in war were rapidly developing. A technical radar

When Clarence H. Giest died on June 12, 1938, in Villanova, Pennsylvania, many Boca Raton residents feared for the future of the club and of their town. Giest, who had subsidized the club's operation from the first, was discovered to have created the C. H. Giest Trust which continued to oversee operations of the facility. The membership learned the extent of Giest's subsidies in a December 1939 letter from the Spanish River Land Company's president, Harold S. Schutt. The Boca Raton Club owed the land company $4,200,000. The land company, in turn, owed the Geist Trust $5,600,000. Schutt said it was clear that these obligations could never be supported by the earnings of the club.

school had been established at Scott Field in Illinois in 1941. By 1942 the rush to train radar operators and mechanics made it evident that a new location with good flying weather all year long was necessary. South Florida provided the ideal weather and also had two other advantages: the boats on the Atlantic shipping lanes supplied good targets for practice runs and since the Army Signal Corps radar school had been established at Camp Murphy on the Loxahatchee River, a nearby location would be advantageous for the exchange of information and personnel. Boca Raton also had a third advantage. Because of Clarence Geist and his general manager Gordon Anderson's work, the town already had an airport. It also had a great deal of land to expand that small facility.

Unfortunately, these many advantages seemed meaningless when Gen. Henry "Hap" Arnold arrived to inspect the site. According to Jackie Ashton Waldeck in *Boca Raton: A Romance of the Past*, a tropical storm left the streets and airfield standing in six inches of water. Nonetheless, the high land west of the airport remained dry and General Arnold recommended the Boca Raton site for the base. The government began the acquisition of property almost immediately. Starting with the air field, the Army acquired a total of 5,860 acres from more than one hundred property owners. Over fifty families lived on the land, many of Japanese ancestry from the former Yamato colony. While the government never confined the Japanese to camps on the East Coast of the United States, many did loose their land to the air base.

Also included within the base's lands which were bound by the Florida East Coast Railway tracks on the east; Palmetto Park Road on the south; and Fifty-first Street on the north, was a community of around forty black families in the area of Fortieth Street. This settlement of houses and shanties, "had been built over a period of fifteen years on land not possessed through legal channels." Delray Beach allowed some of these black families to move their houses to that city. The rest were razed. The government took the land under an act that allowed "emergency condemnation" without an appraisal and before compensation was determined. Among the pioneer families to suffer, Perry and Florence Purdom lost their home as did Bert R. Raulerson, who left Boca Raton, never to return according to Waldeck. The base also included the building at Northwest Second Street and the railroad track operated as a restaurant and tavern by Louis A. Zimmerman. Although a two-story nine-room structure its owners received only $2,500 in compensation because of its frame construction. Zimmerman then opened Zims on Federal Highway, a block south of Palmetto Park Road. The new Zims proved a popular hangout for the soldiers of the base.

Col. Arnold MacSpadden was sent to Boca Raton in the spring of 1942 to supervise construction of the field's buildings and runways. Drollene Brown says he required fourteen contractors, thirty-five hundred construction workers, and $11 million to complete the project. With typical wartime speed, the Boca Raton Army Air Base opened for its first training class in October and by January of the next year three 5,200-foot-long airstrips and over eight hundred structures were ready to receive troops.

As the Army Air Corps' only radar training school during the war years the camp offered classes for electronics and radar officers, as well as courses

covering all related specializations for enlisted men. Beginning with 1,340 men in 1942-1943, the school served almost 15,000 the next year and enrolled 16,281 troops by 1945. Shortages plagued the school during its first years. Although the base had only ten dilapidated English Judson patrol bombers in October 1942, by the war's end one hundred airplanes, half of them B-17s, were assigned to the field.

The Army Air Corps also took over the Boca Raton Club in 1942 to house the officers from among the thousands of trainees. Although hotels from Miami Beach to Palm Beach were commandeered by various branches of the armed forces, few were as luxurious as the Boca Raton facility. Harold A. Turner, who later founded a plant nursery on Federal Highway and served as mayor of Boca Raton, directed the club's grounds staff when the Army arrived. He told an interviewer from the Boca Raton Historical Society how every member of the staff rushed to store the valuable antiques, oriental rugs, expensive paintings, and other elegant furnishings, substituting standard GI bunks and furnishings. When the first officers moved in, four to a room, gray paint covered the walls and padded covers protected pillars and carved plaster

pieces. Turner remembered that unstored items, such as carpets and rugs, all had to be replaced in 1945 when the club reopened.

The airfield population dwarfed the little town of Boca Raton, which never could supply enough civilian employees. Brown says civilians worked in all offices and departments with the largest number required by the academic and quartermaster departments, and the post engineers. When the number of civilians working at the facility rose to fifteen hundred they were drawn from all over the country and, because there was so little housing in Boca Raton, forced to commute from as far away as Fort Lauderdale.

Drollene Brown pointed out that Boca Raton's small size also created problems for the airmen who could find no activities for their free time. Zim's and Brown's, the two bars in town, did a land-office business, as did Max Hutkin's and Tony Brenk's stores. She mentioned that someone converted a garage into a "GI Funhouse" where the "jukebox rarely stopped," and that the officers used the facilities of the Boca Raton Club and the Cabana Club, although an officer's club was later constructed on base. Nonetheless, lines of GI's stretched a mile long in each direction at the little bus

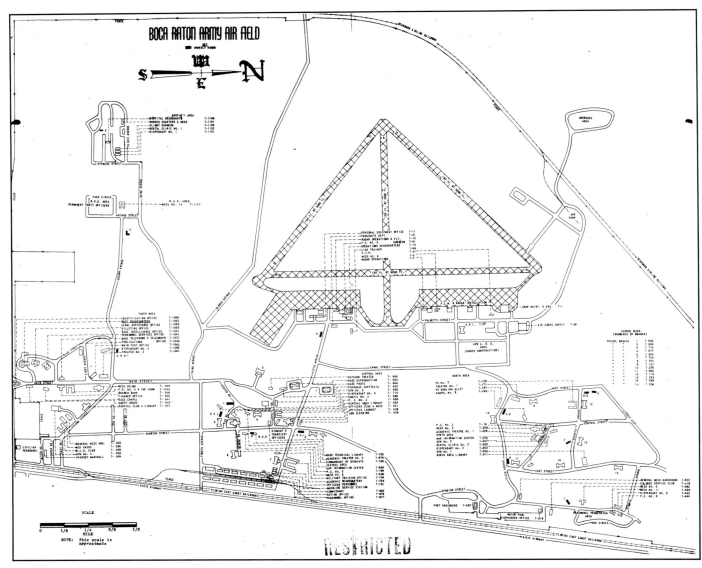

BOCA RATON ARMY AIR FIELD

RESTRICTED

This map shows the main entrance to the Boca Raton Army Air Field at Palmetto Park Road and Northwest Fourth Avenue (labeled Main Street). The many administrative offices of the base were grouped in this area and included the base headquarters, the billeting office, base intelligence office, the post office, telephone and telegraph office, in addition to the chapel, officers' club, and theatre. The sixteen warehouses on the Florida East Coast Railway siding still are in use today. The road running from the right of the warehouses to the runway area is today's Northwest Twentieth Street. The base medical complex can be found at the upper left corner of the map. One source claimed the irregular meandering street patterns were adapted to foil submarine gun attacks on the base. Drollene Brown suggested that the workers were in such a hurry to complete the roads that they built around rocks and trees rather than taking the time to remove them from their path.

station across from Town Hall waiting either to go north to Delray Beach or West Palm Beach, or south to Fort Lauderdale or Miami.

Boca Raton residents met the airmen in the bars and stores, through volunteer work, and when they rented rooms to their wives. In such a small town there were few rooms available, and with gas rationing, commuting from surrounding towns was always avoided. The demand for rooms in Boca Raton was overwhelming. Ella Elizabeth Holst in "The Life of a Boca Raton Woman," told of Lillian Race William's agreement in 1942 to allow a soldier to build an eight-by-twelve cabin on her property to be occupied by his wife who paid five dollars a month rent. In 1943 in a letter to her hometown newspaper in New York, Williams said she had divided her garage into two parts and rented each to Mexican families with young babies, that the small "cabin" rented by the week, and that seventeen people rented space in her small house. "I sleep in a corner of the piazza," she wrote, "and another couple in the opposite side." All together, twenty-five people lived on Williams's small property.

Although the actual battles of World War II never reached American shores, the war could be seen just off the Atlantic beaches in Florida. After the Japanese assault on Pearl Harbor, U-boats of the German Navy began to attack shipping in the Florida Straits in an effort to disrupt the flow of oil from fields on the Gulf of Mexico to the East Coast of the United States. The first sinking came in February 1942 when the *Pan Massachusetts*, carrying 100,000 barrels of oil, went down off Cape Canaveral. In the next few weeks, tanker after tanker sank with great loss of seamans' lives. One tanker, the *Lubrafol*, loaded with fuel oil, was attacked off the coast of Boca Raton. All fifty of her crew members died in the blazing fire that could be seen for miles. Brown said that several crewmen wore life preservers and that their charred bodies floated to shore. These were taken to the little Boca Raton Coast Guard Station at the inlet. Most German attacks came at night when the tankers were silhouetted, like ducks in a shooting gallery, by the lights on shore. To make the boats less vulnerable, the government ordered blackouts. This meant no streetlights, shop window lights, or floodlights, and that houses near the ocean had to install blackout curtains. Even cars were limited to using only parking lights.

There were also many stories of German spies set ashore by the submarines. One common legend tells of local groceries found aboard a U-boat captured by the United States Navy. In reality, the evidence points to only a few spies set ashore in all of Florida, and that these were quickly captured.

As the loss of tankers and lives continued a Civil Air Patrol squadron, the nation's first, began searching the coastal waters for enemy U-boats. A network of spotter stations, placed in specially constructed towers or oceanfront buildings, also kept a watch on the shipping lanes. Volunteer teams of local residents and Army wives manned a watchtower on the Boca Raton beach. At first they searched the shipping lanes for enemy submarines and the beaches for possible spies, later they watched for enemy aircraft. When World War II began the Coast Guard's Gulf Sea Frontier, charged with the defense of the Florida coast, the Bahamas, and Cuba, had only three coastal cutters, a few other inadequate ships, and a number of battered planes.

With the Florida sinkings the Coast Guard received additional support and could organize "killer packs" to go after the U-boats.

After all the losses off the coast, even the most humane Floridian cheered the sinking of a German submarine. The increased surveillance by the Coast Guard and the decision of the German high command to center submarine activities in the North Atlantic ended the activities off the Florida coast by the summer of 1943. Thus by the spring of 1944 the government could terminate the volunteer spotter program, though the watchtower on the Boca Raton beach remained for many more years.

While active fighting left Boca Raton's shores in 1944, the radar school continued its operations as increasing numbers of airmen arrived for training. Among these were several of note. Col. Gus Grissom began his military career at the Boca Raton base as an eighteen-year-old clerk-typist. Twenty years later Grissom became one of America's original seven astronauts. While serving as first commander of Project Apollo he died on January 27, 1967, in a fire in his spacecraft at Cape Canaveral.

The popular singer Tony Martin was perhaps the best-known of the airmen stationed at the Boca Raton field. Brown said that by the time he arrived the Third Air Force Band had also been established. Made up of professional musicians who had played with such musical legends as Jimmy and Tommy Dorsey, Glenn Miller, Artie Shaw, Benny Goodman, and Paul Whitman, the fifty-three member band was able to take to the field on September 22, 1942, after only one rehearsal. As the Air Corps stationed more musicians at Boca Raton they were grouped into smaller units. In these years the Third Air Force Band as well as a symphony orchestra, string quartets, woodwind octets, and dance and jazz bands played engagements all over South Florida.

By the time the war ended, Boca Raton's citizens had become as dependent on the air base as they were on the club in the 1930s. Almost everyone either worked for the Army Air Corps or provided services for its personnel. They also used the base's recreational, entertainment, and medical facilities. Many townspeople feared what would happen should the base close. Some hoped that it might become a permanent field for the training of pilots. Although peace failed to close the base, the numbers of students declined rapidly. Almost four thousand officers,

Boca Raton Army Air Field Headquarters sat on the top of the ridge just to the north of Palmetto Park Road and west of Northwest Fourth Street. Most of the base buildings were completed in a three-month period in 1942. Col. Arnold MacSpadden used thirty-five hundred workers to construct over eight hundred buildings and three gigantic runways. The base headquarters building still stands and is used as an apartment house.

enlisted men, and cadets trained at the base in September 1945. By May 1946 the number had fallen to under twenty-seven hundred. In May of 1947 the Air Force decided to transfer operations of the school to Kessler Air Force Base at Biloxi, Mississippi, by the end of the following November. The move was in progress when a hurricane with 155-mile winds hit the area on September 17. As many base buildings had been hurriedly constructed, in fact, most were officially designated "temporary," the damage was extensive. The estimated three-million-dollar destruction hastened the move to Mississippi and the closing of the Boca Raton Army Air Field.

When Boca Raton's mayor and councilmen realized that the radar school was about to close they decided that the town should purchase the airbase. Mayor J. C. Mitchell declared in 1947 that "Boca Raton wants the air base. . . . We notified the WAA (War Assets Administration), the CAA (Civil Aeronautics Administration) and the U.S. Engineers that this city will . . . acquire Boca Raton Field in its entirety for its own municipal air field." Mayor Mitchell also revealed that he had received inquires from "various agencies" that wished to lease former air base buildings to establish "all kinds of businesses." Mayor Mitchell had brought the Army Air Corps to town to begin Boca Raton's development. Now that the war had ended, he and the town council were determined to continue its growth.

In June 1949 the town agreed to pay $251,284 for the 2,404-acre air base property. In the contract with the WAA Boca Raton promised to operate a civilian airport on the 1,325-acre airport site west of the El Rio

Canal. The town paid for the air base property by immediately selling the 1,079-acre "excess" land east of the canal, although it retained title to the waterworks and sewage collection and outfall system, and to the streets and roads laid out by the Army Air Corps. A section of land south of Palmetto Park Road, where the army built airmen's housing, sold to the St. Joe Paper Company. Ed Ball controlled the company, which like the Florida East Coast Railway, was part of the estate of Alfred duPont, his late brother-in-law. The land north of Palmetto Park Road went to Joe L. Moore of Gadsden, Alabama, who immediately began to lease and sell the property. Because of its gentle rolling terrain, he named his development Boca Raton Hills. Many of the former base buildings became warehouses, small factories, schools, and apartments.

A *Miami Herald* article of the 1950s told of Moore's success in luring business to Boca Raton. Most of the sixteen large warehouses the Army built next to the FEC tracks now served private companies. The Army's meat storage warehouse housed the Colonial Packing Company, a ham processor with facilities for an ultimate output of 1.5 million pounds of meat a week. Four more warehouses contained Karl Philips, Inc., a chicken-raising company using an assembly-line procedure that could produce as many as two million broilers a year. In connection with this enterprise the Philips company also offered for sale two hundred one-acre homesites to the west of the industrial area for development as chicken farms.

Other companies in the warehouses included the Scranton Metal Casket assembly plant, the Wats Manufacturing Company which made tire changers for

This aerial view of the apron area of the Boca Raton Army Air Field shows the base aircraft lined along the southern edge of the pavement. Many of the buildings seen in the upper right-hand corner of the photo are still in use today on the Florida Atlantic University campus where much of the pavement serves for student and faculty parking. The El Rio Canal can be seen in the lower right-hand corner of the photograph.

aircraft and heavy trucks, the Sun and Sea Paint and Varnish Company, which came to Boca Raton after the company's license to manufacture paints was rejected by the city of Hollywood because of citizen complaints, and G. G. Whitehead's printing works.

Fortunately for the image that Boca Raton developed in the 1960s, most of these industrial and agricultural processing concerns proved short-lived. This was not the case in the largest sale Joe Moore made of the old air base land. In 1950 the Reverend Ira Lee Eshleman, a former Detroit clergyman and radio "Bible commentator," purchased thirty acres along both sides of Northwest Fourth Avenue that included several large air base buildings to establish a "winter Bible conference grounds." One building had been the base officers' club. Eshleman later said that he believed from the first that the hilly and heavily wooded area would prove ideal for a conference site. Moreover, he found the buildings vandalized, many of their windows broken, and the grounds littered with rubble. Eshleman believed the poor condition of the property would mean a low price. Then he discovered that a gambling syndicate had bid $50,000 for just the officers' club and four acres of land. Eshleman said he had made a number of friends through his radio program and they now came forward with offers of loans and donations. He bought the thirty acres with Moore giving generous terms and a long mortgage.

When Eshleman began to prepare the buildings for the coming winter season he found people from Miami to West Palm Beach eager to help him. He had no funds for furniture for eighty-five guest rooms and almost gave up when a Miami hotel owner, about to refurbish,

provided the answer. Another new friend had nineteen soda fountain chairs, a refrigerator, and other restaurant fixtures in storage and donated them to the project. A nurseryman, who recognized Eshleman's voice from his radio show, donated six large truckloads of tropical shrubs and citrus trees. Finally, over five hundred people came to the summertime dedication of the Bible grounds.

Over the next few years the conference grounds continued to grow with the the addition of 220 more acres. The new land included the base theatre which was converted into a large auditorium. By 1955 there were facilities for 150 overnight guests with all the amenities expected of a Florida resort: a sixty-foot swimming pool, tennis courts, shuffle-board, and putting greens. Eshleman hoped to retire the large debts he had incurred by developing subdivisions around the conference grounds. He said in 1955 that 210 "Christian people" owned their own building sites and that twenty-five houses were under construction. Plat books still list the names of the various conference grounds subdivisions: Beulah Heights, Conference Estates, Conference Ridge, and Conference Lake Estates. Another subdivision far to the west was named Paradise Palms. Eshleman also claimed in 1955 that the Bible grounds were America's largest winter Chautauqua, and reported that on Sunday nights as many as a thousand people jammed the auditorium to hear the weekly sacred music concert which a West Palm Beach television station broadcasted locally.

In 1962 the Winter Bible Conference Grounds officially became Bibletown, U.S.A., and at the same time Eshleman began a five-year court battle with Palm

Young airmen from all over the country reported to the Boca Raton Army Air Field by the thousands to train as airborne radar operators and radar mechanics. The base was the Air Corps only radar training school. Here engineers continued to develop and refine the new device which was still in its infancy in 1942 when the Boca Raton field opened. Their work was highly classified and the school itself was considered a military secret. Many sources spoke mysteriously of a "radio beam" school and told of how mentioning the word radar was an offense punishable by court-martial.

Beach County and the city of Boca Raton over assessments on the organization's property. Eshleman claimed that everything owned by Bibletown, U.S.A., including the motels, subdivisions, and other business-oriented properties should receive tax-exemption on religious grounds. In 1967 the courts decided that only the property used specifically for religious purposes, such as the auditorium, the school buildings, and the parking lots were exempt from property taxes.

The Reverend Ira Lee Eshleman also retired in 1967. While he had suffered some health problems, Bibletown's $1,700,000 debt and small membership probably account for the early retirement. His successor, the Reverend Torrey Johnson, also told a reporter for the *Fort Lauderdale News* that Eshleman got into trouble because he "sometimes couldn't tell whether he was making money for the church or himself." Nonetheless, during his seventeen years as head of Bibletown, Eshleman brought thousands of people to Boca Raton for meetings, concerts, and services. The widow of the evangelist Billy Sunday came to the conference grounds in the 1950s. Anita Bryant and Charlie Weaver performed in concerts, and Billy Graham brought an "evangelistic rally."

Under Johnson, Bibletown became less interested in real estate sales and promotion and more interested in building a local twelve-month-a-year church. By the late 1970s membership had reached 1,350 and the debt had been reduced to around $200,000. Recognizing the new emphasis the name was changed to Bibletown Community Church. In these years Bibletown also founded Boca Raton Christian School. Originally twelve grades, the high school portion of its program was phased out in the early 1980s. Under Johnson the winter conferences also continued. When the old conference center burned in June 1976 a new $2 million building was quickly constructed. Additional rebuilding has meant that only a few vestiges of the air base remain.

On March 27, 1944, James Carroll, manager of the Roney Plaza Hotel in Miami Beach, made the somewhat startling announcement that J. Meyer Schine of New York, who owned a chain of theatres across the United States and a number of hotels, had purchased the Boca Raton Club and the entire village of Boca Raton. He went on to say that although the Boca Raton Club would be operated as a hotel, no plans had been made "for the rest of the village." The report, published in the *Palm Beach Post*, said that Schine had bought the village from the estate of Clarence Geist and that in addition to the hotel it included a City Hall, Fire Department, service buildings, two golf courses, hundreds of acres of land, and a number of residences.

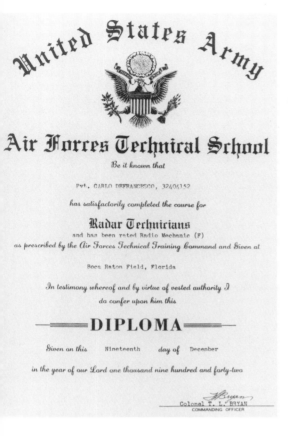

Pvt. Carlo DeFrancesco was one of the earliest graduates of the United States Army Air Forces Technical School at Boca Raton Army Air Field. He received his diploma, which was signed by base commander Colonel T. L. Bryan, on December 19, 1942, which certified that he had satisfactorily completed the course for radar technicians.

Close to two thousand troops can be seen on parade in this photograph looking south over the main apron of the Boca Raton Army Air Field. The soldiers are dwarfed by the gigantic aircraft hangers on the left.

The indignant citizens of Boca Raton responded the following day. In a story entitled "You Can't Just Buy a Village!" the *Post* quoted Police Chief William H. Brown as saying "a person can't walk in, peel off a roll of bills and buy a town—just like that . . . I'm a property owner here, and I'll be darned if anyone's going to come to tell me to pack up and go." The manager of the Boca Raton Club confirmed Chief Brown's statement: Schine had purchased the club, its property, and the Spanish River Land Company, not the incorporated village of Boca Raton.

The mistake made by the Schine interests is easily understood. Certainly Clarence Geist often acted as if he owned the entire village. During the 1930s Boca Raton officials had regularly functioned as Geist's personal employees, asking for his approval for town budgets, proposed improvements, and appointments. Once his general manager, Gordon Anderson, wrote to the town clerk: "I assume you have either a bad case of hookworm or writer's cramp, but, be that as it may, I want information by return mail. . . ." With Geist exercising this type of control over the town, the Schine interests might have been justified in thinking they had bought the town. Actually, by 1944 Boca Raton was no longer the sleepy little village of Geist's day. The coming of the air base had brought a new boom and prosperity. With the Army in town the hotel

seemed less important to Boca Raton's citizens. While the *Post* might claim that they were "clinging grimly to their front porches, armed only with righteous indignation but pledged to battle this monstrous resurgence of free bootery," in reality, a new era of growth had already started.

According to Stanley Johnson in *Once Upon A Time,* J. Meyer Schine had come penniless to the United States in 1903 from Latvia and built a $150 million hotel-theatre-real estate fortune. He picked up the Boca Raton Club for a bargain three million dollars. Although when the air force moved out it hired an architectural team, headed by Palm Beach architect John Volk, to restore the building to its postwar condition, in opening the hotel to the public, the Schine organization decided to "modernize" the building. The bottom half of Mizner's old dining room and the open patio overlooking the lake were combined to form a large new dining room with little character. Mizner's loggia received glass walls, and much of the old carved panels and woodwork were covered with gallons of light colored paint. Furnishings for both the public rooms and guest rooms were replaced with bland institutional pieces typical of the era. Even the great wrought iron chandeliers disappeared. The new Boca Raton Hotel and Club reopened on January 15, 1945, and proved extremely

A gigantic radar antenna on the Boca Raton Army Air Field. The Air Corps chose the South Florida site for radar training for its good flying weather all year long and because the boats in the Atlantic shipping lanes provided excellent targets for practice runs. Moreover, the Army Signal Corps had also established a radar training school just north of West Palm Beach which allowed the two camps to conveniently exchange personnel and technical information.

popular. Over the next few years Schine added to his Boca Raton investment, purchasing many more acres of land and four thousand feet of oceanfront.

The Schines moved to Boca Raton in 1948 and Hildegarde Schine immediately became involved in the community. When she heard that many townspeople "had never sat foot in the front door" of the club she gave a party and invited everybody. Although hundreds of people came, she found them "very suspicious." To counteract this suspicion she joined a group of women who were attempting to found a library. Although the women organized a small library on the second floor of Town Hall, they soon realized the space was inadequate and decided to build their own building. Hildegard Schine said that they then organized the Art Guild to raise money for the library. The women held art shows, gave musicals, and hosted card parties and teas to raise money for the project. Although Schine gave his wife a downtown lot for the library and art guild, she found the parking inadequate and sold the lot for $50,000. This money, in addition to the $85,000 raised through the various benefits, was divided between the two organizations. The library eventually found a home on Northwest Second Avenue and in 1961 the Art Guild moved to Floresta, where many of its founding

members lived. In 1986 the Art Guild changed its name to the Boca Raton Museum of Art.

Hildegarde Schine also teamed with Lavonne Mouw, wife of a Boca Raton contractor, to give a number of musicals to benefit the Methodist Church building fund. She later said the minister told the audience after a concert that the ladies had raised enough money for the church and could now sponsor a new charity. Afterwards, "Mrs. Mouw turned to me and said, 'Well, I guess we've fixed up your church.' 'But,' I told her, 'I'm not Methodist, I'm Jewish!' And I thought she was Methodist, but she wasn't either. She was Presbyterian."

Hildegarde Schine told Geoffrey Lynfield that she also arranged for the making of the best known of South Florida movies. Theodore Pratt, who lived in Floresta, gave her a copy of his novel *The Barefoot Mailman*. When Irving Thalberg and Sylvan Simon, producers with Columbia Pictures visited the Schines at the hotel, she told them how much she enjoyed the book. The producers read *The Barefoot Mailman* and signed a contract that same weekend acquiring the rights to the screenplay.

Theodore Pratt lived in a Mizner cottage in Floresta from 1946 to 1958. It was the most productive period for the writer, often known as the "Literary Laureate" of Florida. Although Pratt wrote articles for magazines

The United States Army Air Corps remained rigorously segregated during World War II. Although blacks were trained in radar operation, their Squadron F had facilities almost completely separated from the rest of the air base. Integration of the armed forces came after the war as a result of directives from President Harry S. Truman.

The radar school instructors are shown with a number of trailers supporting portable antennas and radar equipment. The education department was the base's largest and additional schools developed beyond the basic radar training. These included high and low altitude bombing, radar navigation, airplane identification, attack interception, and survival training. Many of the instructors were civilians.

like the *Saturday Evening Post*, short stories, and a number of lurid sensational novels, *The Barefoot Mailman* remains his best known work. It was the first volume in a trilogy that recounted the history of Southeast Florida from the days of the first pioneers to the real estate bust of the mid-1920s. In the pioneer era of *The Barefoot Mailman*, the area was an unspoiled Eden. The snake entered Eden in *The Flame Tree* in the form of Henry M. Flagler's Florida East Coast Railway which brought people and civilization. *The Big Bubble* told the story of Addison Mizner, his Boca Raton development, and the Florida of the land boom which finally destroyed Eden in the 1920s. In case anyone missed the point, in *The Big Bubble* Pratt named the Mizner character Adam, his wife Eve. Adam named his dream city Roca Faro, and as with the Boca Raton original, lost everything with the collapse of the real estate boom.

Pratt wrote both *The Flame Tree* and *The Big Bubble* in Floresta. In the case of all three novels he conducted

extensive research and interviewed many participants in the events. He first published *The Story of Boca Raton,* which is really a history of the hotel and club, in 1953. It had been printed and revised four times by his death in 1969. Unlike Mayor Mitchell and other town fathers who continued to seek opportunities for Boca Raton's development, Pratt had come to Boca Raton from Lake Worth seeking the isolated Garden of Eden existence he wrote about. Floresta in 1946 remained a heavily wooded area connected to the rest of town by one narrow road. In 1958, still seeking his Florida paradise, Pratt moved to western Delray Beach. In an article for the *Miami Herald*'s *Tropic Magazine* Pratt complained that Boca Raton had "exploded with real estate developments" and that he envisioned the entire state turning into one great metropolitan area.

While Pratt decried development in Boca Raton, others promoted what they hoped would be a new land boom. In February 1949 Harold R. Davis announced his plan to build a one-square-mile planned

industrial community just north of the air base. Davis chose Boca Raton for its central location near sea, land, and air transportation routes. He claimed that the Seaboard and Florida East Coast Railway came closest together at this point, that the Intracoastal and the planned new "super-highway" passed through his land, that the air base bordered on the south, and that the Port of Palm Beach and Port Everglades in Fort Lauderdale provided close contact with the Caribbean. Davis said, "I think all South Florida is rapidly waking up to the fact that this area offers more than resort sunshine; that we need service industry for ourselves; light manufacturing for a sound, year-round economy, and facilities for getting our share of the great

Caribbean market." A Miami Beach real estate man and former president of the Florida Association of Realtors, Davis proposed a project in which the industrial buildings could convert easily to war plants should the need arise. Robert Fitch Smith, a leading Miami architect, provided plans for the industrial park which included prototype manufacturing buildings connected to a central utilities system. Although his plan was the result of a two-year study, Davis failed to gain the financial support needed to build the industrial community.

Other Boca Raton projects, especially those oriented to tourism and the town's resort image, proved more successful. Africa U.S.A., perhaps the largest and most lavishly planned tourist attraction in Florida before Disney World, opened in February 1953. Africa U.S.A. was the dream of John D. Pederson, a contractor and successful Fort Lauderdale real estate investor who for years had carried on a long-distance love affair with the dark continent. Although he never visited his great love, he planned and executed a 177-acre, lushly landscaped park stocked with hundreds of free-roaming non-carniverous African animals. Pederson bought his land, located just to the west of the Boca Raton railway depot and south of Camino Real, in 1950. He then invested hundreds of thousands of dollars during the next three years in preparing what became South Florida's largest tourist attraction.

The first animals began arriving for Africa U.S.A., in the fall of 1952 when Pederson's son Jack returned

The base hospital can be seen on the Boca Raton Army Air Field map isolated in an area far to the west of the other major buildings of the facility. It was the center of a complex of buildings that included nurses' and doctors' quarters, a dental clinic, and a dispensary.

The Boca Raton Army Air Field included dozens of buildings such as this barrack for enlisted men. These barracks were built in all sections of the base and show the temporary nature of much of the construction found on the field. These structures are not shown on the base map.

The Boca Raton Army Air Field chapel was located just inside the main gate on today's Northwest Fourth Avenue. Although a simple wooden structure, there was a dignity in its plainness. After the war the chapel was moved to Delray Beach where it was remodeled and became the First Church of Christ Scientist.

Volunteers staffed a religious center on West Palmetto Park Road that attempted to minister to the needs of the air base servicemen. After the war the center became the Baptist Church and later the Unitarian-Universalist Fellowship. The building, now remodeled into Mediterranean Revival style, houses professional offices. The individuals in the photograph are the local volunteers who ran the center. Standing from the left are Harry Cheseboro, Mr. Everett, the Reverend Linger, Mr. Jones, the Reverend W. A. Croswell, Mayor J. C. Mitchell, and the Reverend Parrot from Deerfield. Seated are Ethyl Cheseboro, Mrs. Everett, Essie Mae Roseke, Mrs. Parrot, and Mrs. Linger.

from a buying safari with a herd of sixty zebras, six Abysinian asses, twenty ostriches, and a pair of cheetahs (which were to be caged). Before the park opened, giraffes, elands, kudus, besas, chimpanzies, elephants, hippopotamuses, and all kinds of colorful African fowl joined the early arrivals. To make these animals feel at home Pederson also planted thousands of tropical shrubs and trees. One source said a sample of the list of plants read like a horticultural catalogue and included royal poincianas, bougainvilleas, hibiscus, and several hundred different kinds of fruit trees from all over the world.

Reporter Ted Gore in the *Fort Lauderdale News* described "a 30-foot waterfall cascading 275,000 gallons of water a minute into a 800-foot stretch of flower-decked rapids leading to a seven-acre artificial lake; a 160-foot geyser which blows its lid every hour and five minutes; miles of winding rivers; acres of grassy plains, and patches of natural dense jungle." Visitors viewed the exotic animals from small motorized trains modeled on streamline diesels and stopped at a mud and thatched native village where they could have their photograph taken with the fierce Masai warriors.

Signs up and down the entire East Coast directed visitors to Boca Raton and Africa U.S.A. The park, probably the first safari attraction in the United States, proved extremely popular and gained several thousand paid admissions daily. Pederson appeared with Jack Parr on the "Tonight Show," to bring still more publicity to Boca Raton and his park. The August 1, 1960 issue of *Life*, then still a mass-circulation weekly pictorial, carried a cover picture of the Boca Raton attraction. The story, on American "theme parks . . . aimed at being educational," gave equal coverage to Africa U.S.A. and California's new Disneyland.

Just over a year after the *Life* article, Africa U.S.A. closed. While remaining popular with tourists who enjoyed the "sociable safari," the park fell victim to rising land values of the fast growing Gold Coast and the African red tick. Residents of a new housing development to the south of the theme park complained of the traffic and noise. Other new subdivisions west of the attraction petitioned Boca Raton city fathers to extend Camino Real westward into their area. To acquire the right-of-way, some Africa U.S.A. property was condemned. Then in May 1961, federal agricultural agents discovered African red ticks at the tourist attraction. The ticks, the first ever discovered in North America, created a panic. Agricultural agents threw a quarantine line across the southern end of the peninsula, and ordered thousands of dollars worth of Africa U.S.A. animals destroyed.

On September 4, 1961, Pederson closed the gates of Africa U.S.A. for the last time and offered the land and the animals for sale. Within a month he found a buyer

for the land. Powdrell and Alexander, Inc., a development company from Rhode Island, agreed to his million-dollar-plus price tag for the 177 acres. He also collected $180,000 in animal sales to various zoos across the country. Almost immediately work began to turn the "simulated jungle" into a site for 450 houses. Although the subdivision, named Camino Gardens, retained part of the old attraction as a park, the rest was leveled, replaced by canals, streets, and lots which were "manicured, pedicured, and replanted." Some of the African fowls eluded Pederson's efforts to capture them. Residents of the new Camino Gardens often found peacocks in their gardens, and Muscovy ducks became as common in Boca Raton as pigeons in other cities.

At about the time Pederson opened Africa U.S.A., another, although more modest tourist attraction, opened at the north end of Boca Raton. In the late 1940s, E. G. Barnhill of Fort Lauderdale, described by one source as a wealthy treasure hunter and adventurer, bought twenty-four acres of land north of Fifty-first Street between Federal Highway and the Intracoastal Waterway. The site contained a number of Indian burial mounds which dated from between A.D. 700 and 1300. Barnhill invited Ripley P. Bullen, an archaeologist with the Florida State Museum at Gainesville, to investigate the largest mound. Bullen and his wife, anthropologist Adelaide K. Bullen, excavated the twenty-foot high mound during the fall of 1954. They found seventy-two Indian "bundle burials." Bullen said the Indians placed their dead in a burial house, and after a number had accumulated, they buried the bones in neat bundles in the mound. Skulls were often placed on top of the bundle. The Bullens

said the burial mound belonged to a Caloosa village located about a quarter of a mile away on the shores of Lake Wyman.

A later investigation in 1971 by Professor William Sears of Florida Atlantic University's Anthropology Department confirmed most of the earlier findings, although he found the mound had been used by early Tequesta Indians, a fish-eating people who lived along the lower southeastern coast of Florida and had an extremely primitive culture. Although these Indians subsisted mostly on shell fish, Sears said they caught sharks, eating the meat and using the teeth for arrow tips. He also found evidence that they constructed tools from conch shells and bone. The Tequesta Indians disappeared long before the arrival of the first white settlers. Sears believed that Spanish slave hunters rounded them up to work the Caribbean sugar plantations.

Barnhill decided to exploit the site and opened a tourist attraction called Ancient America. A mission-style building on Federal Highway contained a large hall with murals showing the first meeting between the Spanish and the Indians. The hall was also the attraction's museum, displaying pirate chests, Spanish gold, armor, old canoes, shrunken heads "and many other authentic articles." Naturally, there was also a store selling tourist souvenirs.

Behind the main building the tourist could visit the "partly" restored Indian village site and walk through a tunnel in the twenty-foot high burial mound which contained exhibits of Indian life. The Barnhill displays suggested that the Abanika Indians, a sun-worshipping branch of the Caloosa, had built the mounds. Their name was romantically translated a "Children of the

This photograph is looking north on Federal Highway. Zim's Bar can be seen at Royal Palm Way on the left and the tower and cupola of the Town Hall is just beyond. The Boca Marine Building is on the right. This photograph is a visual representation of why the airmen felt there was nothing to do in Boca Raton.

Dawn." It was later claimed that the site also contained remains of a Spanish Mission or of a chapel built by Spanish navigators.

To attract the attention of tourists speeding down Federal Highway, Barnhill constructed a thirty-foot-long concrete boat, allegedly modeled after the ship "Ponce de Leon sailed to Florida in his quest for the Fountain of Youth." The ship lasted much longer than Ancient America. In 1958, Barnhill closed the attraction. Bitter about its failure, he said, "I opened the place so people could understand some of the history that took place in Boca Raton before it was ruined. . . . It seems that all everyone is interested in down here is dog tracks and horse races." Business had been so bad in 1958 that he claimed, "if we had put up a sign reading 'Smallpox, keep out' we would have had the same number of visitors at the end of the year." Barnhill retained ownership of the site for several years after Ancient America closed. Then increased real estate taxes forced him to sell the property to Boca Raton developers Marqusee Associates.

In 1968 local historians attempted to interest state officials in at least twenty acres of what became known as the Barnhill Mound Site for a state park. They proposed that the property be purchased with state and federal funds and then they would raise money for a museum building from "prominent people." In 1973 David Ashe, a city councilman and chairman of the newly organized Boca Raton Historical Society, led a new fight to save the mounds. He convinced the council to petition the Florida Internal Improvement Fund, consisting of the governor and cabinet, to purchase the Barnhill Mound Site. While a purchase of historic property in Palm Beach County was approved, County commissioners chose mounds

Located just north of the Boca Raton municipal golf course, this oceanfront tower was one of a series of World War II spotter stations along the southeast coast of Florida. Volunteers, drawn from town residents and the wives of air base personnel, manned the station twenty-four hours a day on the lookout for enemy submarines and aircraft. A Boca Raton News story said the tower contained a telephone so the volunteers could call the air base when they spotted a plane. Abandoned as an observation post in 1944, the tower was razed in 1949 or 1950. With the dawn of the space age in Florida, a radar tower was built on the site in the late 1950s. The new tower was part of NASA's downrange tracking system for missile launches from Cape Canaveral. Later the tower was leased to Georgia Tech for a period and then in 1978 it was razed and a condominium built on the site.

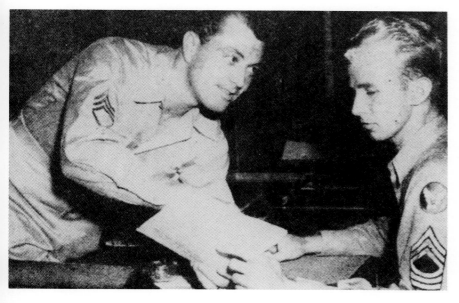

Staff Sergeant Tony Martin was one of the more prominent servicemen to be stationed at the Boca Raton Army Air Field during World War II. This unidentified newspaper clipping from the files of the Boca Raton Historical Society shows a young soldier who seems happy with his new assignment. The air base's many musical organizations and their concerts gave the citizens of the town great pleasure during the war years.

When the September 17, 1947 hurricane hit the Boca Raton area many airmen had already been transferred to their new radar training facility at Kessler Air Force Base in Mississippi. In a Boca Raton News interview in 1974 Col. Arnold MacSpadden, who supervised construction of the Boca Raton base said that the plans called for all buildings to be of frame construction. MacSpadden found lumber scarce, and even when he could find it, the size and kind were often wrong for the job. As he had orders to complete the work as soon as possible, he used concrete blocks as a substitute. Many of the block buildings are still standing in sections to the east of the Florida Atlantic University. Frame buildings, such as the Post Stockade, failed to survive the hurricane.

near the J. W. Corbett Wildlike Management Area over those in Boca Raton. When the Sanctuary subdivision was built its owners agreed to preserve the large mound, though it is now closed to the general public.

The success of Mayor J. C. Mitchell in bringing the Army Air Corps Radar Training School to Boca Raton and the building of the gigantic air field, convinced the town's leaders to continue to promote development in the years after the war. They encouraged commercial ventures and new housing subdivisions and pledged to place Boca Raton in the forefront of growth. The goals of the town fathers were aided by the thousands of servicemen who had been stationed in Florida during the war. After a winter or two in their old homes in the north, many decided to return to Florida to live. While Boca Raton remained relatively undeveloped and unknown through the 1950s, its discovery was only a matter of time.

The 1947 hurricane winds blew the enlisted men's barracks off their foundations and crushed them like toys. Although these barracks were the most numerous buildings on the entire base, none exist today.

135

Joe L. Moore of Gadsden, Alabama, came to Boca Raton after World War II to purchase the land and surplus buildings of the air field. With the encouragement of Mayor J. C. Mitchell and the Town Council he promoted industrial and business development, leasing and selling the surplus base warehouses and other buildings to commercial ventures.

The 1947 hurricane caused massive destruction on the air base and flooding in other parts of Boca Raton. Now that the hurricane had passed, these Floresta neighbors laugh about the eight inches of water surrounding their houses. In the 1940s Floresta remained isolated from the rest of the town, almost completely surrounded by unused portions of the air base and general wilderness. Roberta MacSpadden, wife of Col. Arnold MacSpadden, the builder of the base, later told of almost stepping on a large rattlesnake in her Floresta garden.

Boca Raton sold the Garden Apartments to the St. Joe Paper Company in 1946 for $70,000. The company, part of the Florida empire of Alfred duPont which also included the Florida East Coast Railway, was controlled by his brother-in-law, Ed Ball. After trading hands several times over the next few years, the property had deteriorated greatly and was seen as a major eyesore in downtown Boca Raton.

Joe L. Moore purchased most of the surplus Boca Raton Army Air Field land east of the El Rio Canal. He immediately began marketing the land and the surplus buildings, naming his development Boca Raton Hills. He advertised the buildings as "suitable for commercial, industrial, hotels, motels, hotel court apartments, multiple-family dwellings, warehousing, wholesale, retail and light industry." Certainly, home sites at five dollars per front foot would be considered a bargain in contemporary Boca Raton.

Domina C. Jalbert came to Boca Raton in the late 1940s to establish an aerology laboratory on Northwest Twentieth Street in an old air base building. Here seen with one of his early kites on a deserted street, Jalbert gained world fame for his kite, sail, balloon, and parachute designs. A success story among the many organizations using the surplus base properties, Jalbert's "parafoil" changed the entire concept of kite and parachute design. Based on the air-glide principle of the airplane's wings, the parafoil's air-filled cloth wing-shaped design, once called mockingly "flying mattresses," were the most radical departure in parachute design since Leonardo da Vinci according to Life Magazine. The parafoil kites, which had no frame, required less wind to fly than a regular kite.

The Sjostrom Machine Company, one of the many manufacturing enterprises to establish their operations in the former buildings of the Boca Raton Army Air Field, made textile machinery. Many of these well-built concert block buildings continue to serve Boca Raton business.

Soon after he established his aerology laboratory in Boca Raton, Domina C. Jalbert began work on scientific barrage balloons for the armed services. Jalbert is seen in the center inflating a Navy test balloon. His Kytoon, half-kite and half-balloon furthered the Jalbert Aerology Laboratory's experiments with air currents and atmospheric conditions. The laboratory's many colorful kites and balloons were a familiar sight in the sky over Boca Raton for thirty years.

The entrance of Thy words giveth Light

One of the largest sales of surplus buildings and land from the Boca Raton Army Air Field made by Joe L. Moore was to the Reverend Ira Lee Eshleman for his winter Bible conference grounds. Moore, described by Eshleman as a "Christian businessman" agreed to both a low down payment and a long-term mortgage. The Harry A. Ironside Memorial Auditorium had formerly been the base theatre.

The Harry A. Ironside Memorial Auditorium became the setting for many religious services as well as sacred music concerts and popular programs by well-known entertainers. Both Anita Bryant and Charlie Weaver performed at the Winter Bible Conference Grounds. For a number of years a West Palm Beach station televised a weekly program from Boca Raton.

The Winter Bible Conference Grounds brought hundreds of people to Boca Raton each year since its founding in 1950. The Administration Building housed the organization's offices and was formerly an air base structure.

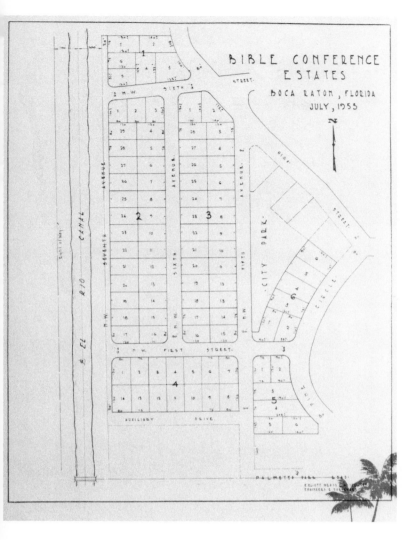

In order to meet the costs of the Winter Bible Conference Grounds, Eshleman began selling building lots to visitors who wished to live in a Christian setting. This Plat for Bible Conference Estates shows building sites and streets just to the west of the main buildings of the organization. The area labeled as a park was later divided into additional lots.

This large Boca Raton Army Air Field building stood just inside the main gate on Northwest Fourth Avenue and was part of the base's administrative offices. It was purchased by the Reverend Ira Lee Eshleman for his Winter Bible Conference Grounds. Known as Moody Hall in honor of the Evangelist, it was used as a cafeteria and apartment house until the 1980s.

The Reverend Ira Lee Eshleman with Billy Graham during one of the evangelist's many visits to Boca Raton. Eshleman, who founded his Winter Bible Conference Grounds in 1950 in buildings of the former Boca Raton Army Air Field, remained president of the organization until 1967. He later said it was America's largest winter Chautauqua providing Bible-study classes and evangelistic services in a resort-like setting.

Before the Army Air Corps took over the Boca Raton Club in 1942 it was one of the most exclusive private clubs in the United States. It had been able to maintain that exclusiveness because owner Clarence H. Geist had spent freely of his own fortune to develop it and to subsidize its operation. By 1944 the Geist Trust officers realized the club would never be profitable and so they sold it to hotel-movie theatre-real estate magnate J. Meyer Schine who announced that once the Air Corps officers had moved out, the facility would reopen as a hotel.

J. Meyer Schine purchased the Boca Raton Club from the C. H. Geist Trust in 1944 while the Army Corps still used it as quarters for officers training at the airfield. Although recognized as one of America's most exclusive private clubs, Schine paid only three million dollars for the clubhouse, Cabana Club, the golf courses, and several hundred acres of property.

The Boca Raton Municipal Building expanded to house additional firefighting equipment purchased to augment Old Betsy, seen here painted white. Boca Raton attorney W. F. Finch promised that the town and all of its officials were dedicated to providing all necessary services for its growing population.

Three of the hardest workers among the volunteers to fund and build both a library and art guild were Helen (Mrs. Richard) Mann, Hildegard (Mrs. J. Meyer) Schine, and Eleanor (Mrs. W. P.) Bebout. Hildegard Schine's donation of $50,000 helped the two support groups to purchase property and begin operations. The Art Guild built on Palmetto Park Road in Floresta while the library was located in what is thought of as the downtown government complex.

A reception was held at the Wavecrest Way home of Lavonne Mouw on March 15, 1955, after a musical benefit for the Methodist Community Church of Boca Raton. Shown with members of Tony Cabot's band are Mrs. Mouw on the left and Hildegard Schine behind the church-shaped cake. Mrs. Schine later told that both women worked to raise money for the church thinking the other was a member.

Theodore Pratt wrote many of his historical novels about Florida life in his Mizner bungalow in Floresta. He came to Boca Raton in 1946 when the city of Lake Worth become "too congested." He moved to western Delray Beach in 1958 still seeking a quiet rural setting after the postwar boom started in Boca Raton. He later said that Florida's constant growth would soon have him "marching through Georgia." Pratt is shown with some of the material he donated to the Florida Atlantic University.

Florida Atlantic University.

In the late 1940s Boca Raton's downtown still had more vacant lots than buildings. Looking up Federal Highway the Cities Service gas station is in the lower left, on the south side of Palmetto Park Road. On the north side is the Standard Station, the Town Hall, and on Boca Raton Road is Tony Brenks store, now the Haggerty Building. Boca Raton Road marks the northern boundary of the built-up area of downtown Boca Raton.

Local beauty queen Dorothy Steiner, in the center, seen here participating in a contest at the Cabana Club. Although there is no information about this photograph, the contest probably had nothing to do with Cinderella. Steiner went on in 1953 to become Miss Florida. Later she was runner-up in the Miss America pageant in Atlantic City.

In the 1940s, Doctors still carried black bags and made house calls. Shown here is Dr. William G. O'Donnell in front of his office on Boca Raton Road. Dr. O'Donnell came to Boca Raton in the 1930s as physician in residence of the Boca Raton Club. Both he and his wife Dorothy became active in community affairs. Dorothy ("Dottie") O'Donnell started the town's first mimeographed newspaper, the Pelican.

The volunteer crew of Boca Raton friends who helped each other and the community when help was needed. This group had painted the Lion's Club and now was repairing and painting the Eubank house. From the left standing are Bill Eubank, Ray Hillegas, Johnny Olsson, and Roy Roseke. In front are Johnny LaMont, Earl Trammell, "Spider," and Lew Harris. In the early 1950s, Boca Raton remained a small neighborly town.

This young tourist shows no fear for the fierce Masai warrior found at Jungle Town in Africa U.S.A. Although a thriving tourist attraction, developmental pressures and the discovery of the African red tick forced its closure in September 1961. John Peterson sold the property and animals for over a million dollars and moved to Australia.

Hundreds of non-carniverous animals greeted visitors to Africa U.S.A. The three-car fifty-passenger rubber-tired trains traveled the miles of roadways allowing the passengers a close-up view of the free-roaming animals.

This aerial view of Boca Raton, taken around 1960, shows the still undeveloped Africa U.S.A. on the right side and in the middle of the photograph. The canals and first houses of Boca Islands can be seen just above the park and the beginnings of the subdivision to its west. Although Camino Real extends west beyond the photograph, Palmetto Park Road ends at Northwest Twelfth Street.

147

The tragic death of Debbie and Randy Drummond in the spring of 1962 convinced many Boca Raton residents that the city needed its own hospital. Four months after their death, their mother formed the Debbie-Rand Memorial Service League when eighteen local women met in her Camino Real home. This grew to almost two thousand volunteer-members who helped raise the funds to build the Boca Raton Community Hospital which was dedicated on June 25, 1967.

Boca Raton Community Hospital

C H A P T E R   V

ARTHUR VINING DAVIS AND THE ARVIDA YEARS

When Clarence Geist owned the Boca Raton Club, walls and guards protected it from the surrounding community. During those years Boca Raton remained a small farming town which provided services and labor for the club. During the 1960s this image of the poor town surrounding the wealthy and exclusive club changed completely. When Arthur Vining Davis purchased the hotel in 1956 he also acquired over a thousand acres of land. Almost immediately he set out to transform the town. In the next few years well-planned, lavishly landscaped, and expensively priced subdivisions changed Boca Raton's image forever. By 1972 a *Miami Herald* reporter could call the town "a rich man's playground, a haven for the affluent."

Arthur Vining Davis first began purchasing land in the Bahamas and South Florida in the late 1930s. As chairman of the board and a founder of the Aluminum Company of America, also known as Alcoa, Davis acquired a great fortune, estimated as high as $350 million. America's growing air power in World War II produced a huge new market for aluminum for the production of airplanes. Davis guided his company through a multimillion-dollar expansion program which included building the world's largest smelter on the Saguenay River in Canada. The town the company founded near these works honored its chairman. Its name, "Arvida," was produced by using the first two letters of his names.

After the arduous and exhausting labor of the war years, Davis decided to spend more time in Florida. He owned land in the Bahama Islands and many acres in South Miami, and had also purchased Journey's End, an estate in Coral Gables. He spent lavishly in remodeling the Spanish Revival-style house, and even paid to move Old Cutler Road when he discovered that the traffic with its noise and headlights intruded upon his privacy.

Davis, called by *Look* magazine "a short, peppery, hawknosed, sharpeyed, whitehaired, publicity-hating man," was born in Sharon, Massachusetts, in 1867. After attending the Roxbury Latin School, he graduated Phi Beta Kappa from Amherst College in 1888. His father, a Congregational minister, then found him a job in Pittsburgh with Charles Martin Hall, who developed the process for cheap production of aluminum. He assisted Hall on Thanksgiving Day in 1888 when the first commercial aluminum was produced. When sixty years later the eighty-one-year-old Davis moved his headquarters to Miami in 1948, his Pittsburgh associates seemed justified in believing that he planned to retire. Instead he instigated an acquisitions program that added thousands of acres of land to his already large holdings. By 1956 he owned close to one-eighth of Dade County, 25,000 acres in Broward County, property near Tallahassee and St. Augustine, more than 20,000 acres on Eleuthera in the Bahamas, and 200,000 acres on Cuba's

Director of Public Works William Prendergast and former Councilman Andrew Brennan examine the first modern garbage packer purchased by the Town of Boca Raton in 1955. At the time the Chamber of Commerce estimated the town population as 2,736. By the end of the decade 6,961 people lived in Boca Raton. As the population rose, city fathers decided to convert to a more efficient form of government. On September 17, 1957, a new charter adopted the city manager-commission form of government and changed the name from Town *to* City *of Boca Raton.*

Isle of Pines. At the same time Davis bought or started a number of businesses, including an ice cream factory, airlines, cargo ships, a road-building concern, and a bank. When Floridians, awed by this wholesale purchase of their state, asked why the buying binge, Davis answered, "I buy properties with the thought of making money." Freeman Lincoln, writing in the September 1956 *Fortune* magazine concluded, "that all his acquisitions . . . are based on a conviction that inevitably, and reasonably soon, there must be a huge appreciation of the value of real estate." Obviously, the Alcoa chairman believed South Florida was ripe for a new boom.

In July 1955, Stuart I. Moore, a Palm Beach County hotelman who had worked for J. Myer Schine at the Boca Raton Hotel and Club, asked Davis to back him in the purchase of a Delray Beach hotel. Davis backed his purchase in this and other Delray Beach properties and also made Moore his assistant. A few months later, Moore told Davis that Schine might be interested in selling the Boca Raton Hotel and Club. After a January 1956 inspection trip, the Alcoa chairman approved negotiations which ended in late February with the $22,500,000 purchase of the hotel, golf club, Cabana Club, a partially completed shopping center, and a mile of beachfront land that extended from Palmetto Park Road to the Broward County line, which with some other town property equalled around fifteen hundred acres. Schine, who had paid the Geist heirs $3 million for their entire Boca Raton property just twelve years earlier, retained the land north of Palmetto Park Road.

At the time of the sale, the *Boca Raton News* said the club had two hundred permanent and six hundred seasonal employees. The permanent employees, mostly residents of the town, operated the Cabana Club during the summer months and maintained the extensive

properties owned by the club. The new owner of the hotel and club organized his holdings and about five thousand acres of land he acquired to the west of town into Boca Raton Properties, Inc., and placed Moore in charge of a gigantic improvement project. In July a thirty-five man crew began round-the-clock, seven-days-a-week dredging operations at the inlet. When this was completed both jetties were extended, the lake was deepened to ten feet, and a new marina was constructed. Moore also supervised interior renovations to the hotel. The Cathedral Dining Room received a spectacular refurbishing with five thousand square feet of gold leaf applied to its ceiling and columns. The *Delray Beach Journal* said this created "a brilliance breathtaking in splendor when contrasted to the deep tones of the Royal Purple carpet and drapes designed and woven especially for the job." At the same time, sixteen murals depicting the history of polo were painted for a new restaurant called the Polo Lounge.

Just as Davis approved the gilding of the hotel's interiors, so he now directed a gold edge be returned to its reputation. In 1958 he brought L. Bert Stephens, a professional hotel man, to modernize the facility and upgrade its image. In the following years the hotel received numerous awards, including the highest "5-star" rating from the *Mobile Travel Guide*. Davis also named Sam Snead, summer golf pro at the famed Greenbrier Hotel, winter pro at Boca Raton. Adding even more polish to the image, Moore also announced that beginning in January 1957, polo would come to Boca Raton. This both justified the naming of the Polo Lounge and, according to James McGoldrick, an officer of Davis's company, proved "our willingness to make a sizeable investment" in Boca Raton. He also claimed that polo, more than any other project, would bring "the right kind" of publicity to the hotel and town.

Council members Frank Roadman, owner of Boca Raton's first department store, and George Whitehouse, proprietor of the Whitehouse Motor Lodge on Federal Highway, discuss charter changes with Mayor William O'Donnell, center, on the steps of old City Hall in 1957. O'Donnell, who pushed for charter reforms in Boca Raton's government was successful, although his administration lasted only one year.

The Boca Raton Hotel groundskeepers laid out a 450-by-1,000-foot playing field, built bleachers and boxes, and prepared a parking lot on Camino Real on the grounds of the south golf course. For the first two seasons, the horses, stabled at the old Phipps' field in Gulf Stream, were transported to Boca Raton for the Sunday afternoon matches. The Boca Raton team fielded many internationally known players including two nine-goalers. For the first few years Russell Firestone, Jr., also played for the team. Davis, a high-goal polo fan, personally presented the Arthur Vining Davis Trophy each year.

For the 1960 season the matches moved to an eighty-nine-acre site west of the airfield on Glades Road. To prove the claim that Boca Raton was the "winter capital of polo," Davis invested a half million dollars in two "emerald green grass playing fields;" an exercise track; a "stick and ball" field for practice; stables for 146 horses; living quarters for trainers, grooms, and exercise boys; and a lounge and locker room for the players. For almost two decades, winter Sunday afternoons found the citizens of Boca Raton at the polo field, the day often a benefit for a local charity. Although most members of the audience had never attended a polo match before coming to Boca Raton, they soon learned to purchase champagne from the cart, picnic from their tail gates, and run onto the field to stomp divots back into place.

Davis also polished Boca Raton's image by promoting new luxury housing subdivisions. Milton N. Weir,

president of the real estate company bearing his name and chairman of the Delray Beach National Bank, became developer and sales agent for Davis's Palm Beach County properties. Florida bankers and real estate interests pointed out that Davis's large land purchases had created a boom. At the same time they criticized his lack of long-range development plans for his holdings and claimed that his death could result in the selling of much of the property, forcing a panic in the market. Weir's appointment and the announcement of development plans helped to quiet the criticism, as did the creation in 1958 of the Arvida Corporation. Davis placed his land holdings and the Boca Raton Hotel and Club into the new corporation and named Weir its president. While retaining a majority of the company's stock, Davis sold the rest in a public offering.

The public stock sales created the capital for the $5 million developmental costs of Royal Palm Yacht and Country Club. The plush subdivision, located between the Intracoastal Waterway and Federal Highway just south of the hotel grounds, helped establish a new rule for the Boca Raton real estate market: "The bigger and more expensive they are the better they sell." For Royal Palm the Arvida Corporation built a $200,000 clubhouse, an eighteen-hole golf course designed by Robert Trent Jones, a $500,000 yacht club and yacht basin, and spent $1,250,000 placing the electrical utility system underground. The Miami architect Robert Fitch Smith designed all the club buildings. The

Arthur Vining Davis with his longtime secretary and companion Evelyn Mitchell (on the right) in his box at the Royal Palm Polo Field. After his purchase of the Boca Raton Hotel and Club in 1956, Davis immediately began a program to renovate the property and polish the image of both the town and hotel. Polo, the sport of princes and kings, was introduced during the 1957 season when Davis constructed a playing field with bleachers and boxes across Camino Real from the hotel.

The former Alcoa chairman, and owner of the Boca Raton Hotel and Club, presented the Arthur Vining Davis Trophy in 1964. Davis, a polo fan, often attended the matches in Boca Raton. With the development of the Royal Palm Yacht and Country Club, Davis invested half-a-million dollars to move the fields to a site west of the old air base on Glades Road. Beginning in 1960 Sunday matches on the "emerald green" playing fields became a Boca Raton tradition.

development, taking its name from the stately royal palms lining Camino Real on its northern border, was also the first Boca Raton neighborhood with guarded entry gates. The 742 homesites were priced from $10,000 to $45,000 and most fronted either water or the golf course. Even Arvida officials expressed surprise when the most expensive lots sold out first. Both the luxury and expensiveness of Royal Palm Yacht and Country Club set the new standard for Boca Raton.

As Arvida worked to polish Boca Raton's image with its exclusive subdivisions, others saw the city developing as an educational center for South Florida. In fact, for a few years in the 1960s the incorporation sign at the south limit of the city on A1A read: "Boca Raton, The Cambridge of the South."

The Florida legislative session of 1955 authorized the Board of Control, the governing body of the state higher education system, to begin planning for a new university on the Southeast Florida coast. The air base at Boca Raton, largely deserted since the 1948 hurricane and the moving of the radar training school to Mississippi, seemed to many the perfect university site. Its 1,250 acres allowed for future expansion and

its location in south Palm Beach County near the Broward County line meant the new university could conveniently draw students from the entire southeast coast. Nonetheless, a Broward County site committee and another from central Palm Beach County also pushed locations in their areas.

The Board of Control finally selected the old air force base when the Broward Committee recommended the Boca Raton site and when consultants pointed out that it had a potential of 30,000 students within an hour's drive. Thomas F. Fleming, Jr., had lead Boca Raton's campaign to bring the university to the air base site. He now had to convince the federal government to give the state title to the land.

Fleming, although Georgia-born, came to Florida as a child. His father, Thomas F. Fleming, Sr., an attorney and later president of the American National Bank, moved his family to Fort Lauderdale in 1924. After graduating from Fort Lauderdale High School the younger Fleming attended the University of Florida. At the Gainesville campus his fellow students elected him president of the class of 1938, and selected him for membership in Blue Key, the leadership honorary. Other Blue Key members included George Smathers, the future senator, and Paul Rogers, later a congressman.

Fleming moved to Boca Raton after his marriage to Myrtle Butts, daughter of August and Natalie Butts, in 1939. He became actively involved in the management of Butts Farms and served on the Town Council. In 1956 he founded the First Bank and Trust Company, today part of NCNB bank. From the first he supported his town and the cause of higher education in Florida. When the Board of Control chose Boca Raton for the university site, Fleming used his friendship with Smathers and Rogers to make the contacts that gained an agreement with the Civil Aeronautics Administration granting a thousand-acre tract for the university. The agreement which went into effect in March 1960 stipulated that the state had to establish a university on the site by 1969. The slightly more than two hundred remaining acres of the air base site were set aside for a civilian airport.

While Fleming negotiated with the federal government, the Board of Control began planning the new university. A planning committee headed by Dr. A.J. Brumbaugh, a well-known authority on higher education, consulted scholars from many fields. The "Brumbaugh Report," issued in June 1961, called for an upper division university of juniors, seniors, and graduate students that would complete the work of the public junior colleges of the state. Through the use of extensive media aids and technology, a faculty made up of "master teachers" were to gain time for greater individual contacts with students and for their own research projects. The technology included a "learning laboratory" with television channels, an automated library, and student "work stations," taking advantage of both audio and televised information sources, spread around the campus. This plan was devised before the development of the small inexpensive computer.

The state cabinet, sitting as the Board of Education, approved the building of Florida's fifth state university in Boca Raton on May 9, 1960. It also set September 1964 for the opening of the institution. Unfortunately, the state legislature still had refused to vote funds to build the school. Panhandle "pork choppers" in control of the legislative process demanded a new university in Pensacola before one in South Florida.

In order to start the planning process for the physical plant, the Board of Control called upon the Boca Raton community to raise $100,000 for planning and architectural fees. In 1959 the county had created a university committee with Fleming as chairman. This committee now decided to raise the planning money.

In a 1960 Sanborn Square political rally, Democratic gubernatorial candidate Farris Bryant pledged his complete support for the new university and promised to find construction funds. During the rally Fleming gave Bryant a membership card for the "Boca U in '62 group established by his committee to raise funds. Fleming also helped establish the Endowment Corporation to pay architectural fees for campus buildings, and salaries for the president and other officials before the university opened. He pledged a minimum of 1 percent of First Bank and Trust earnings before taxes to the corporation, which raised $284,669 by 1964.

After his election as governor in 1960 Bryant realized that all the state universities desperately needed additions to their physical plants. He then called for the issuance of $25 million in bonds to build the Boca Raton campus and aid the other institutions. After a long court battle, in July 1962 the state sold the bonds and the new university in Boca Raton received $5.3 million for construction.

With the building of the campus assured, the Board decided the university now needed a name. Over the years the community most commonly applied the nickname Boca U to the institution. The Board wanted a name that applied to the entire southeastern Florida region. Since a campus in the central part of the state had been named the University of South Florida, a location name seemed ruled out. After a newspaper poll that received such suggestions as Palm State, Peninsula University, Gulfstream University, Kennedy University of Florida, and in honor of the space program, A-Okay University, the Board of Control settled the issue by adopting Florida Atlantic University at its May 11, 1962 meeting. At the same meeting it also named the fifty-one-year-old president of Miami-Dade Community College, Kenneth Rash Williams, as the university's first leader.

Williams, a native of Monticello, Florida, received his bachelor's and masters degrees from the University of Florida and his doctorate from Chicago. After various positions at the Universities of Georgia and Florida, he became president of Florida Junior College in Ocala. There he became a friend of Ocala native Farris Bryant, who had known Williams' wife Selma since childhood. In this period friends pushed Williams' candidacy for the presidency of the University of Florida, though

During the Second World War while governor-general of the Bahamas, the Duke of Windsor often visited Florida. Later he made annual trips to Palm Beach, often staying with the Robert Youngs. In the mid-1950s the duke and his duchess were lured to the Boca Raton Hotel and Club to attend the Heart Ball. The duke, an avid golfer, was perhaps brought to Boca Raton by the promise of a round with golf pro Tommy Armour, on the right. Fred Perry, the hotel's tennis pro, seems to have captured the dukes's attention.

rumors claimed Governor LeRoy Collins blocked his appointment, citing his lack of scholarly attainments. Williams became the founding president of Miami-Dade Community College in 1960. Now his friend Governor Bryant saw him appointed to the $16,500-a-year job as president of Florida Atlantic University. Williams arrived on the Boca Raton campus July 1, 1962, and set up his offices in the air base's converted fire station.

While Tom Fleming raised money for the new state university, his brother-in-law Harold Butts, helped establish a second educational institution in Boca Raton. The Episcopal School Foundation, under the leadership of Father Hunter Wyatt-Brown, founded Saint Andrew's School in 1961. Arvida contributed forty acres from its undeveloped University Park land and Butts gave the school an adjacent ten acres. Opening in 1962 as a boys' school with grades seven through twelve, its reputation as the area's leading college preparatory institution grew quickly, as did its campus and physical plant.

Alexander D. Henderson, a former Avon Products executive, became a major benefactor. The school's administration building bears his name and the chapel of Saint Andrew the Apostle is a memorial to him. Russell Rooks, Brouwer D. McIntyre, Albert H. Surprenanat, and the Arthur Vining Davis Foundation all contributed additional buildings to the campus.

These buildings, in Bahamian Colonial style, with an Olympic-sized swimming pool, tennis courts, and eighteen acres of playing fields, set amidst small lakes and a landscape of pine and tropical shade trees gave the school one of the most beautiful campuses in the state. When the Miami Dolphin's football team used it as a training camp in the late 1960s, it was called "the finest pre-season camp in football today."

The Episcopal School Foundation established a girl's preparatory school in the mid-1960s. Saint Ann's was first housed in a vacant condominium on A1A. Later it was moved to an oceanfront hotel in South Palm Beach. Unfortunately, it never enjoyed Saint Andrew's success, and after it closed Saint Andrews became coeducational in 1971.

In September 1963, a full year before the opening of Florida Atlantic University, another institution of higher learning welcomed its first students. Marymount, one of five colleges of the Religious of the Sacred Heart of Mary, provided a "two-year college education for young women who show promise of achievement at this level." An all-purpose academic building, named for Miami's Bishop Coleman F. Carroll, a student center called Founders Hall, a dormitory, and utilities building were ready for the first class. The sixty-five-acre campus, just north of Glades Road on Military Trail, contained room for the planned future expansion

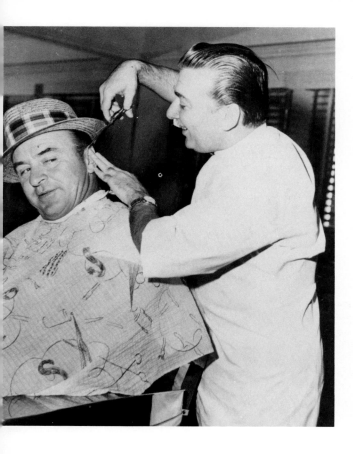

In an effort to upgrade the sports image of the Boca Raton Hotel and Club, Arthur Vining Davis hired Sam Snead as the new golf pro. "Slamming Sammy" refuses to remove his trademark hat, even when receiving a hair trim from hotel barber Louis Andinolfi.
Photograph by Jim Leo

which included additional residence halls, an administration building, chapel, library, convent, and recreational facilities. Mother M. Joques became the institution's first president, although Mother de la Croix, who had directed the campus building program, soon succeeded as head of the institution.

Mother de la Croix, christened Mildred O'Connell on her birth in Chicago, saw the student body grow to around five hundred during her administration. In the late 1960s the college added a large new library-learning resources building with carrels where students could listen to tapes programmed to supplement their classroom work, and two addition dormitories with accommodations for five hundred students. She was also responsible for pioneering what Marymount called "the block study approach" in the liberal arts program. A student concentrated in each of four areas for a seven-week period. These included theology and philosophy, natural science and mathematics, history and human behavior, and humanities and art.

Unfortunately, innovative teaching techniques, new programs such as secretarial science and radiological technology, and even the admission of men failed to bring enough students to make the school financially successful. In 1971 Wilmington College, of New Castle, Delaware, took over the struggling Boca Raton

institution. After changing its name to the College of Boca Raton, the Wilmington president, Donald Ross, took over as head of the new non-sectarian school. In 1974 the college added the third and fourth years to its program and began conferring baccalaureate degrees.

When Thomas Fleming attempted to raise the money to build Florida Atlantic University, he discovered how woefully inadequately the state of Florida supported the entire university system. He believed that in order to attract the high technology and clean industry that the state needed for development that a first-rate university system had to be built. To campaign for the passage of a constitutional amendment to allow a $75 million bond issue for the improvement of higher education, Fleming became chairman of a Florida Chamber of Commerce group called "Citizens for Florida's Future." The Boca Raton civic leader spoke all over the state for the amendment and secured the endorsements of Senators Smathers and Spessard L. Holland. The amendment passed in the November 1963 election. In a speech before the Florida Chamber of Commerce meeting in Tampa, President John F. Kennedy praised Fleming for his work. It was Kennedy's last public speech before he flew to Dallas.

The original five campus buildings were complete in June 1964. On Sunday afternoon, June 21, ten thousand visitors toured the new library, science

Boca Raton residents actively worked to build Bethesda Memorial Hospital in Boynton Beach. This group of fundraisers proudly display the architect's rendering for what will be South Palm Beach County's first hospital. Mary Ghotto, Joyce Mitchell, Mrs. Bert Rogers, Jr., Elsie Laird, Margaret Olsson, Jean Mitchell, and Libby Vassen pay close attention as Dorothy O'Donnell points out the hospital's many features.

laboratory, television, classroom, and utility buildings. Later that same week the administration, faculty, and staff began moving into their new campus offices.

From the first, the original staff understood that the state of Florida had no intention of providing the funds necessary to create the institution envisioned in the Brumbaugh Report. As Roger H. Miller, the first dean of administrative affairs pointed out in his memoirs, "The seed of experimentation, rather than being nurtured was, from the very outset, treated like a bonsai tree, pruned to the edge of extinction." Nonetheless, planning continued for courses utilizing television and other innovative techniques. When most of the new faculty members arrived in August they eagerly joined this planning process. The slogan chosen for the university, "Where Tomorrow Begins," seemed an appropriate description.

Although classes were scheduled to start on September 8, hurricane Cleo hit the Florida coast and postponed the opening until September 14. Original projections predicted twenty-five hundred students enrolling in fall 1964. Officials scaled this back to two thousand during the summer, and as September approached there was growing apprehension that far fewer might actually attend. Nonetheless, no one dreamed that less than eight hundred students would enroll. The failure of the university to provide dormitories or eating facilities on campus, the shortage of rooms and inexpensive apartments in Boca Raton, the lack of public transportation coupled with the

exceedingly poor South Florida road system, and the insufficient effort to recruit, all contributed to the disappointingly small number of students.

Once more Thomas Fleming supplied the high point in those first months of the university's life. As Florida chairman for Lyndon B. Johnson's re-election campaign, Fleming brought the president to Boca Raton to speak at the October 25 ceremony dedicating the university. In his speech before a crowd of over 15,000, Johnson demanded "a new revolution in education" which would open the doors of colleges and universities for all who could qualify. President Johnson also received the university's first honorary degree. Three weeks later at his official inauguration as president, Kenneth Williams conferred the second on his old friend Governor Farris Bryant. At this same ceremony the university also recognized Thomas Fleming's work and dedication to Florida Atlantic and higher education in the state by awarding him its first Distinguished Service Award.

Williams served as president of FAU for eleven years. In 1973 the Board of Regents named Glenwood Creech, the vice president for university relations at the University of Kentucky, as FAU's second president. Creech's great successes came as a fundraiser. The legislature initiated a program whereby the state added $400,000 to every $600,000 raised to fund Eminient Scholar Chairs. Under Creech the university received the Charles E. Schmidt Chair in Engineering, the Dorothy F. Schmidt Chair in the Performing and Visual

Arts, the Charles Stewart Mott Chair in Community Education, and the Eugene and Christine Lynn Chair in Business. At the time of his retirement his friends also founded the Glenwood and Martha Creech Chair in Science. The university also received a number of endowed professorships and major gifts for specific projects, such as Thomas Fleming's bequest of sixty-three paintings of Florida artist A. E. "Beanie" Backus, the gift of Lullis and Rolland Ritter to build the art gallery, and Esther B. Griswold's many gifts to the Music and Theatre departments. The Dorothy F. Schmidt Chair has been held by theatre legend Joshua Logan, playwright Edward Albee, and actors Hume Cronyn and Zoe Caldwell.

During Creech's administration the university fought for its life through several Florida legislative sessions as proposals to merge FAU with Florida International University in Miami or the University of Florida in Gainesville were debated. In this period FAU also made a commitment to provide more classes and full degree programs in Broward County. After ten years as president Creech retired in 1983. His replacement, Helen Popovich, was the first woman to hold a university presidency in the entire state system. After much discussion, FAU added freshmen and sophomore classes in 1984, ending the upper-division university experiment. Popovich championed the university's affirmative action program and under her encouragement more women and members of minority groups joined the Florida Atlantic University faculty and administration.

In December 1986 Popovich was forced to demote two of her vice presidents after a state university system auditor found evidence of mismanagement at FAU. Much criticism resulted when both men returned to teaching duties, taking their high administrative salaries with them. A little over a year later Popovich resigned and then accepted the presidency of Ferris State University in Michigan. The Board of Regents named Anthony J. Catanese, dean of the University of Florida's College of Architecture, as Florida Atlantic's fourth president.

In 1961 Brown L. Whatley, an Alabama native described as the "personification of southern gentility and dignity," became president of Arvida. Whatley, a principal partner in the Jacksonville mortgage banking and real estate development firm of Stockton, Whatley, Davin and Company, directed Arvida's further real estate development for over a decade. A pioneer in helping to establish condominium ownership, he shepherded condominium legislation through the Florida legislature and during his tenure with Arvida saw the firm build five luxury condominium apartment houses around the shores of Lake Boca Raton and on the oceanfront.

During Brown Whatley's term as president he also directed a modernization program at the hotel which included the twenty-six-story tower, exhibition hall, and large convention center. When the new tower opened in December 1969, at 300 feet it was the tallest occupied building between Jacksonville and Miami (the vertical assembly building at Cape Canaveral was an exception). Designed by a consortium of architects that included the firm of Warner, Burns, Toan and Lunde of New York; Toro Ferrer of San Juan, Puerto Rico; and William Cox, a Boca Raton native practicing in Coral Gables, the new facility cost $11 million. The architects' work, which

By the 1960s old City Hall could no longer house Boca Raton's growing municipal offices. A new City Hall, designed by architect Victor Rigamont rose at the site of the old Geist waterworks on West Palmetto Park Road. Mayor Harold Maull presided at the 1964 dedication ceremony on the front steps of the new building. Councilman Sidney Brodhead and Arthur Mirandi are seated behind the mayor, while band director Philip Azzolino is to the right of the podium.

This is part of the crowd that attended the 1964 dedication of the new City Hall on West Palmetto Park Road. In just two decades the new building proved inadequate. When it was enlarged, city fathers decided the 1960s-modern structure was unrepresentative of the architecture associated with Boca Raton. The new additions and remodeling of the old building were designed in a modern version of Mediterranean Revival style.

they termed "Neo-Spanish-Mediterrean" and Neo-Mizner, enhanced the hotel's reputation for glamour and luxury. Among its 257 rooms, the most luxurious was the presidential suite on the twenty-fourth and twenty-five floors. Its five bedrooms and baths, living room, dining room, library, kitchen, and maid's room were connected by both stairs and private elevator. Although the duplex suite was priced at $750 per day, it was booked through the season. The Hotel and Club's most luxurious restaurant occupied the entire glass-enclosed top floor of the tower.

After Davis's death in November 1962 his trustees sold his 60 percent interest in Arvida to the Pennsylvania Railroad Company. Shortly afterwards the Pennsylvania combined with the New York Central in the greatest railroad merger in history, only to collapse in 1970 in the largest bankruptcy, at the time, in history.

Arvida, still property rich and virtually untouched by the problems of the parent company, continued its

many Florida projects. In 1972 Charles E. Cobb, Jr., a California developer, became president of the company. He quickly established a management group that included John Temple, a former associate from California who became Arvida's president with Cobb's promotion to Chairman. William Shubin, another Californian, headed Arvida's commercial and industrial developments and would later create the company's Park of Commerce in Boca Raton. This team soon embarked on an aggressive development program. The largest of the new projects was Boca West, a 1,400-acre subdivision that included both low rise condominiums and single-family residences in a lushly landscaped country club setting. Located just east of the Florida Turnpike and north of Glades Road, the complex's modern wood and glass clubhouse, golf courses, and tennis facilities proved that Arvida was committed to luxury developments, even in what was then considered far western Boca Raton. Other western

Ball diamonds, shuffleboard courts, and playground equipment were placed in the park just west of the new City Hall along Crawford Boulevard. William Prendergast, director of public works, and James Rutherford, parks and recreation director, seem unable to interest a young client in a duck swing. Prendergast was public works director for over a quarter of a century. Rutherford, who rose from director of parks and recreation to city manager, served the city of Boca Raton for thirty-four years.

projects from this period included Estancia, Paseos, Timbercreek, Millpond, and Town Place.

In 1976 Arvida decided to build a hotel at Sable Point, on the beach just north of the inlet. This was the location where Mizner in 1926 had planned his Ritz-Carlton hotel. Many residents believed the inlet land should become a park and opposed the hotel. When City Council approved the Arvida permit in August 1976, a group of citizens who opposed the council's action, primarily because it failed to allow for public access to the beach on the north side of the inlet, succeeded through a petition drive to force an election on the issue. Although voters approved the council's agreement, five residents, including former mayor Norman Wymbs and council member Ann Cassady, filed suit to block construction, claiming that the public acquired the right by custom to use the beach even though the land was privately owned. The circuit court denied this contention in June 1978 and ground was immediately broken for the new hotel.

The strikingly modern glass and concrete structure designed by Edward A. Killingsworth of Long Beach, California, contained 212 rooms, three dining rooms, and five bars. When it opened in late November 1980 an Arvida spokesman called it the "sparkling diamond" in the "jewel-studded crown" of the Boca Raton Hotel and Club. Named the Boca Beach Club, it provided guests with "exquisite furnishings and the best of everything in service." A motor launch that shuttled

guests between the old hotel and the Boca Beach Club was named *Mizner's Dream.*

While Arvida officials saw the Boca Beach Club as the realization of Mizner's dream, those who worked to save Sable Point disagreed. Ann Cassady called it a "dump." She said, "when you think of what was there . . . . They destroyed a really beautiful piece of nature when they put up that hotel. It's an abortion, what's there now." She also was determined to continue her campaign to save more of the beach front for local residents.

With the opening of the Boca Beach Club, Arvida announced that it planned to close and raze the old Cabana Club. The new hotel was designed to provide the facilities of the now fifty-year-old Cabana Club for hotel guests and club members. Over the past years the Cabana Club had been the victim of "benign neglect." Now it had pealing paint, rotting wood, and leaking roofs. Boca Raton citizens fondly remembered the great steak cookouts, the almost unending food found on the luncheon and Sunday brunch buffet tables, and the wide-open expanse of beach. Cassady proposed that local residents buy the property and restore the club. She said Arvida wanted the thousand feet of beach to put up another expensive condominium. She pointed out that the public had a ten-foot access strip to the beach which might be moved, making the beach completely private. An Arvida spokesman said, "It would be too major a job to restore the club, the entire wooden portion would have to be rebuilt from the

While still governor of Georgia, Jimmy Carter visited the Boca Raton Hotel and Club. Although the group he met with is unknown, the hotel regularly played host to banker, publisher, and investor groups which brought prominent speakers to their meetings.
Courtesy Jim Leo

ground up." When no one stepped forward to buy the club, the bulldozers arrived on January 8, 1981. Although club officials saved items for use in other parts of the hotel, and even talked of finding momentos for oldtime club members (one asked for an old porcelain urinal), only the porte cochere of the structure found a new home. Arvida gave the covered entranceway to the Boca Raton Historical Society. The society moved it to the new county park on the south side of the inlet, the only remaining reminder of the old Cabana Club. As Cassady predicted, the old Cabana Club site became the location for Arvida's most luxurious beachfront condominium project. The Addison, named for Addison Mizner, consisted of two fifteen-story towers with 178 apartments.

In 1981 Penn Central decided to sell Arvida. Its asking price of between $400 and $500 million found no buyers in what turned out to be a depressed real estate market. The next year it dropped plans to sell the company and determined to dispose of various assets instead. In the spring of 1983 Arvida sold the Boca Raton Hotel and Club to VMS Realty Partners of Chicago. VMS paid $100 million for the hotel with its book value of $55 million and appraised value of $80 million. Moreover, Arvida signed a long-term contract with VMS to continue to manage the hotel.

Later in 1983 Charles Cobb and his Arvida management team, backed by the billionaire Bass brothers of Texas, bought the company from Penn Central for $196 million in cash and a $7 million note. In order to reduce the buy-out debt, the new management sold various properties. As a product of one these sales, Crocker and Company received the land to build its upscale Crocker Center office, retail,

and hotel complex on Military Trail in western Boca Raton.

Only a few months after Arvida executives completed their buy out of the company they were approached by the Walt Disney Company. Disney, planning an expansion of its real estate operations, believed that Arvida's management experience would make it an excellent fit for this new program. By May 1984 Disney agreed to acquire Arvida for $214 million in Disney common stock. Tony Ettorre in *Arvida: A Business Odyssey* said that many members of the Arvida management team believed they could make a major contribution to Disney and that Cobb believed "he could ascend to the top of Disney's executive ladder in a short time." Moreover, all the manager/owners of Arvida realized that the Disney takeover meant an immediate financial windfall.

While Arvida proposed development schemes for Disney, it also continued to advance its own projects in Boca Raton. When it sold the Boca Raton Hotel and Club to VMS Realty Partners, Arvida retained much of the land surrounding the resort's grounds. One project of the Disney years was a new condominium development called Mizner Court on the Intracoastal Waterway at the old north gate to the hotel grounds. The five-story development designed by William Cox in "Neo-Mizner" style contained apartments costing from $250,000 to over $600,000.

Unfortunately, the "fit" seen in the early days of Disney's acquisition of Arvida never really worked. Disagreements over management between Disney heirs and major stockholders and the resolution of a hostile takeover attempt with "greenmail," led to the ouster of Disney's chairman and president and the appointment

Although the Reverend Henry Mizner conducted Episcopal church services in Boca Raton in 1926, Episcopalians waited until 1953 to establish their first congregation. Saint Gregory's early small group of communicants quickly grew. In 1956 it built a church on Boca Raton Road and the next year the congregation gained parish status. A decade latter continued growth demanded a larger church. The Right Reverend Henry Louittit, bishop of South Florida; the Right Reverend James Duncan, suffragan bishop of South Florida; the Reverend R. Bruce Ryan, Saint Gregory's rector; and the Reverend Don Marietta, Episcopal chaplain at Florida Atlantic University are seen at groundbreaking ceremonies for the new church which was designed by Howard McCall, AIA.

Governor Ruben Askew, in center wearing a light-colored suit, traveled to Boca Raton in the early 1970s for the dedication of the new Fortieth Street Bridge over the Intracoastal Waterway. The bridge, Boca Raton's third, was the first high-level waterway crossing. To the right of Governor Askew is Boca Raton banker Thomas Fleming, and next to him City Councilmen William Archer, Jr., and William Miller.

of Michael Eisner as the new chairman and chief executive officer. The new management, from the entertainment side of the industry, was less sympathetic to the development proposals from Arvida than the old. Neither did it appreciate Cobb's interests in rising to the top of Disney's executive suite. Although Arvida proposed a major new plan that included comprehensive mixed uses for Disney's projected new community near Orlando, Disney's new management refused to accept the creative plans. By this time Arvida executives had come to see Disney's management as hidebound and bureaucratic.

Given the strained relations, Disney's decision to sell Arvida came as no surprise. In early 1986 an inquiry from Florida Power and Light about Arvida's availability brought an asking price of $400 million, or almost double what Disney paid two years earlier. When Florida Power and Light talks collapsed over the price, Disney management proposed spinning off Arvida in a $400 to $450 million master limited partnership. In such a partnership, units in the partnership are publicly

traded and profits or losses are passed on to the partners. Cobb opposed the plan, saying that Arvida would be forced to earn $40 to $45 million a year for investors to receive a 10 percent return. This earning would leave no money for future expansion.

Cobb then proposed an alternative master limited partnership in which Arvida management and Disney would retain a 17 percent stake in the company. Disney seemed to agree to this proposal and Shearson Lehman Brothers was retained to prepare a $300 million public offering. Then in early 1987, Disney announced that it planned to sell Arvida to JMB Realty Corporation, the giant Chicago real estate syndicator. JMB had earlier purchased Arvida's interest in Town Center, a regional shopping mall in western Boca Raton that Arvida built in cooperation with Federated Department Stores. Now JMB agreed to pay $400 million for the entire company. Cobb said Disney's decision to sell came as "a total shock." Other Arvida officers felt the decision culminated a relationship filled with "back-stabbing, vindictiveness and political battles." One Arvida

Local banker Thomas F. Fleming, Jr., can be called the founding father of Florida Atlantic University. Fleming, who grew up in Fort Lauderdale and attended the University of Florida, came to Boca Raton in 1939 after his marriage to Myrtle Butts. When the state legislature authorized a new university for Southeast Florida he convinced the state university system to choose Boca Raton's old air base for the new campus, talked the federal government into giving the land to the state for the university, and then raised the money to pay planning costs and salaries for the first administrators.

executive said, "I think Disney saw the JMB deal as a way to stick it to us and Chuck in particular." Disney also said that it would not honor a stock option plan for Arvida executives set to take effect in November 1987 since by then the company would belong to JMB. As $30 million in options were at stake, threats of suits, and counter suits immediately resulted. Although much ill will resulted, Disney finally settled for a rumored twenty to thirty-seven cents on the dollar.

JMB, which in 1987 managed real estate valued at $16 billion, had been founded in 1968 by Robert Judelson, Judd Malkin, and Neil Bluhm. In the early years they pioneered the public syndicate business, seeking lawyers and doctors as clients. Later large brokerage and insurance firms also became clients. With diversified holdings that included shopping centers, hotels, apartment, industrial and office buildings, and cable television companies, they became the real estate managers for retirement funds, endowments, and major foundations. Bluhm and Malkin, who had been college roommates at the University of Illinois, bought out Judelson, a Boca

Raton resident, in 1973. The two remaining partners were reputedly worth a billion dollars each.

Most of the members of the management group Charles Cobb had organized for Arvida left the company even before JMB took it over. Their profits from the Disney sale, and the rising value of Disney stock (one estimate claimed the $6 million that Arvida managers invested with the Bass brothers in 1983 in the buy out was worth $250 million in Disney stock by 1987) allowed many of them to embark on development projects of their own. While many had come to Arvida from California or the Northeast, most remained in South Florida. Cobb created a real estate investment and finance company called Cobb Partners with offices in Miami. Many members of the old management group became partners. Cobb was also appointed assistant secretary of commerce for United States trade development and later made ambassador to Iceland. John Temple became president of Temple Development Company in Boca Raton and William Shubin also headed his own Boca Raton development company. Among his projects was the Via Mizner office complex on Federal Highway at Camino Real.

In the fall of 1989 the Boca Raton Hotel and Club changed its name to the Boca Raton Resort and Club and announced a $75 million expansion and modernization project. Claiming that its twenty-year-old convention facilities no longer could complete with other resorts in Hawaii and California, the hotel planned a new 100,000-square-foot convention hall with thirty-five meeting rooms, a 279-room all-suite hotel, a large parking garage, and fitness center and spa.

Then in early 1990 the *Miami Herald* revealed that an investment banker had traveled to Tokyo to look for a buyer for the resort. According to the *Herald* article, the Tax Reform Act of 1986 ended tax breaks that had drawn investors into real estate partnerships. This created numerous problems for VMS Realty Partners, owners of the resort, who now needed cash. Although unconfirmed by VMS, rumors placed the asking price on the resort and club at $250 million.

Over the years, Arvida's interest in western Boca Raton included industrial and commercial as well as residential development. In 1966 Arvida made one of its earliest and most important sales for the history of Boca Raton, to International Business Machine Corporation which purchased 550 acres just west of the Seaboard Railway track and the route for the new Interstate highway. Although at the time IBM claimed it bought the site for "possible future expansion," in March 1967 Thomas J. Watson, Jr., the company's chairman, played host to a breakfast for area business leaders and announced the immediate construction of a 300,000-square-foot facility to manufacture one of the company's large computers.

IBM began manufacturing in rented buildings even before the completion of the first sections of its monumental Marcel Breuer-Robert Gatje-designed complex. Breuer, one of the leading architects of the twentieth century, received his training at Germany's famed Bauhaus under Walter Gropius early in the 1920s. After graduation he joined the school's faculty. With Hitler's rise to power Gropius left Germany, eventually becoming director of the School of Architecture at Harvard. He invited Breuer to join the Harvard faculty and the two began collaborating on the design of numerous projects. When Breuer left the Harvard faculty to establish a private practice he retained the concept of collaborative work in the design of modern structures. Robert Gatje, who had joined his firm, collaborated in the 1960 design of IBM's research center at LaGaude in France. The buildings they designed for the French site, on a rugged slope just ten miles from the Cote D'Azur, were now adapted to the flat terrain of western Boca Raton.

The local facility, begun in 1967, contained low profile manufacturing and warehouse structures and three-story laboratory and administrative buildings which surrounded a large man-made circular lake. Tree-like, Y-shaped columns supported precast two-story-high panels with deep projecting fins designed to protect the windows from the harsh Florida sun. Breuer could make the Boca Raton buildings much deeper than those in France because of "American acceptance" of space without daylight.

The Boca Raton facility remained just one of many IBM plants making computers until August 1980 when William C. Lowe, manager of the Entry Level Systems Unit, convinced company management to support the design of a small desktop computer. While IBM had attempted to enter the desktop market in the 1970s, its 5100 series machines had proven an embarrassment and were quickly withdrawn from the market. Lowe now proposed a new machine, using components and software developed by other companies that would be "user friendly" like the Apple, the major competition in the desktop field.

When the company approved a prototype machine, put together by a task force of handpicked engineers, they gave Lowe only slightly longer than a year to have the product ready for the market. Usually, working within the massive bureaucracy of the firm, such a product might take four to six years from prototype to launching. Lowe put together a twelve-man team headed by Philip "Don" Estridge, an electrical engineering graduate of the University of Florida who had spent his entire career with IBM. This team designed the machine, arranged for its manufacturing, planned the marketing strategy, and developed the advertising campaign all in just a year's time.

Almost everyone connected with the project gave full credit to Estridge for meeting this demanding schedule. James Chposky and Ted Leonsis in *Blue Magic: The People, Power and Politics Behind the IBM Personal Computer*, said that while "being six-feet four inches tall didn't hurt," it was his "style and attitude that made him outstanding." Others remembered his "charisma," and "magnetism," combined with his "regular sort of guy" quality. His ability to see the full picture, assign responsibilities, and then give credit for a job well done created intense loyalty within the team and a strong determination to meet the deadline.

The IBM PC, or personal computer, introduced in August 1981, became the centerpiece of the company's automated office strategy. With the decision to market the machine through Sears Business Centers and the Computerland chain of stores, and to advertise it in a campaign featuring a Charlie Chaplin-like character in a spotless white office with one red rose, Estridge could then sit back and watch sales skyrocket. He quickly rose from director of the development unit to president of the newly formed Entry Systems Division. Under Estridge the work force in the automated Boca Baton factory developed by his research team reached 9,600, and sales of the PC totaled more than $4.5 billion.

Some executives at the Armonk, New York headquarters of the company questioned the need for so many new employees, saying Estridge created an overhead structure that made Boca Raton too costly for manufacturing. John Opel, who succeeded Thomas Watson, Jr., as chairman of IBM had supported the Boca Raton project and its freedom from company bureaucracy from the first. Since the PC was seen as an office machine, Opel now wanted to enter the home computer market. Estridge's new duties as president made it impossible for him to shepherd the machine through to completion. The team designing what became the PC Jr lacked the leadership to meet its deadlines and to hold down costs on the small computer. The high cost of the machine, and what was soon discovered to be only a slight market for a home computer, lead to the PC Jr's failure. Nonetheless, some Armonk executives saw Estridge, and his division's isolation from the company, as responsible for the PC Jr fiasco.

Estridge and his wife Mary Ann had just purchased and remodeled a 1920s Mizner house in Old Floresta when the company joke that says IBM means "I've been moved," came into play. Although saying it was in no way a demotion, IBM brought Estridge to Armonk to become vice president for international manufacturing. The Estridges had just found a new house in New Canaan, Connecticut, when both died in the crash of a Delta Airlines plane at Dallas on August 2, 1985.

William Lowe, who had originated the PC project, became the new president of the Entry Systems Division. By this time John Akers had succeeded John Opel as corporate chairman. While Opel had allowed some experimental decentralization and autonomy on the division level, Akers believed in centralization of the decision-making process. Many Armonk executives believed that the Entry Systems' great success had created too much autonomy for the division. Thus in June 1985 Lowe and two hundred of the executive staff from Boca Raton received transfers to an IBM facility in Montvale, New Jersey, only a few miles from Armonk. Although the automated PC assembly facility at Boca Raton was unaffected, decision making and administrative activities for the once maverick division could be closely watched from corporate headquarters.

Three years later in the summer of 1988 IBM ended manufacturing at the Boca Raton facility and cut sixteen hundred positions from the local payroll. While the company centralized manufacturing at its Raleigh, North Carolina plant, claiming this placed the finished product closer to its market, Boca Raton remained the

Founded by the Religious of the Sacred Heart of Mary, Marymount College opened in September 1963. Located on Military Trail just north of Glades Road, the 65-acre campus offered young women the first two years of their college education. The flooded campus and University Park golf course at the top of the photograph show the effects of September 1964 hurricane Cleo.

division's research and development center. In addition to the Entry Systems Division, the IBM facility in Boca Raton also contained the Applications Systems Division which developed robotic systems and computers used to monitor and control manufacturing, the Communications Products Division which developed telecommunications products for IBM's small and mid-sized computers, the National Distribution Division which marketed personal computers, and the National Service Division which serviced IBM products. Consequently, even though many positions were lost, fifty-five hundred people remained in IBM's employment in Boca Raton.

While still Boca Raton's largest employer, IBM had also fostered the establishment of numerous other local computer companies and suppliers of products and services for "Big Blue." Lance deHaven-Smith, of Florida Atlantic University's Joint Center for Environmental and Urban Affairs, said IBM "put South Florida on the map with respect to high technology." "If Boca was good enough for the nation's biggest computer manufacturer, it was good enough for other companies, too," according to Ed Lopez, the *Miami Herald* business writer. Some of the other large companies that did locate facilities in Boca Raton included Siemens Information Systems, part of the giant German company, and Japan's Sony corporation.

While the city continued to develop and its western area surged with new projects, some Boca Raton citizens began to question this unbridled growth. By 1972 estimates placed the city's population at over 40,000, more than forty times greater than that of only a quarter of a century earlier. Some older, conservative residents believed the continued growth endangered the gracious tranquil life that had made Boca Raton their choice as a winter home or for retirement.

A very young Mother de la Croix became president of Marymount College in 1964. A European historian by training, the new president soon found that her principal job was fundraising. She is seen here speaking to a breakfast meeting with banker Thomas Fleming, far right, sitting at the head table. In a 1970 interview Mother de la Croix told of the fresh ideas and new currents sweeping through the Catholic church. She said that several nuns of the Marymount teaching staff had given up their vows and that she never tried to "encourage any of the departing nuns to remain." Within just a few years she too had returned to secular life.

In October 1964, President Lyndon B. Johnson arrived to dedicate Florida Atlantic University. The ceremony took place out-of-doors on a beautiful sunny Sunday afternoon before a crowd of thousands. Johnson, who was in Florida campaigning for re-election, had Thomas Fleming as his state campaign manager. He received the university's first honorary degree. President Kenneth R. Williams stands behind the podium. On the right is John DeGrove, then chairman of the Department of Political Science; Roger Miller, the first dean (later vice president) of administrative affairs; and a sober President Johnson.
Florida Atlantic University

Younger and more liberal citizens saw the havoc and destruction that unrestricted growth had caused in Dade and Broward counties and vowed to keep it from happening in Boca Raton. Although their motivations differed, the two groups worked together to shape a charter amendment to impose a 40,000-dwelling-unit "growth cap" on the city.

City Councilman Norman Wymbs, who supported the growth cap, failed to convince fellow council members. When Wymbs introduced an ordinance calling for a referendum on the cap at a July 1972 council meeting it failed to receive a second. Earlier a group of citizens gave council a report on the impact of growth on the resources and population of the city. The report detailed the social and economic consequences of rapid growth and specifically mentioned the problems for the water supply and school system. Many of these citizens, angered by

council's failure to support the ordinance, now organized as Citizens for Reasonable Growth. Led by concerned environmentalists such as Roy Thompson, an IBM analyst, and Dorothy Wilken, head of the Florida Atlantic University graphic's department, the new group organized a petition drive to force the referendum. While needing only twenty-eight hundred signatures, Citizens for Reasonable Growth collected five thousand in less than a month.

As the petition drive neared its end, a pro-growth opposition also began its campaign. The executive director of the Florida Atlantic Builders Association called the proposal "vague" and said it raised "serious questions relating to the rights of private property and confiscation by government." An Arvida vice president called the cap "confiscatory, unconstitutional, exclusionary and economically unsound." While various builders' groups and developers echoed these

As the Florida Atlantic University campus developed it came to look less and less like a former air base. Nonetheless, the old runways kept the university from one of the gravest problems faced by other American institutions of higher learning: there was always sufficient parking space. This 1978 photograph shows the campus before the addition to the library and the construction of the new science, engineering, and social science buildings.
Florida Atlantic University

arguments over the next few months, other opponents took up the exclusionary theme, calling the proposal a conspiracy to raise property values and to keep new people out of the city.

In the November election, the voters approved by 7,722 to 5,626 the charter change which limited the legal dwelling units in the city. Even before the election the building department began to receive large numbers of requests for new building permits. In order to allow city officials to work out the density reductions necessary under the cap, the council decided to impose a moratorium on the issuance of building permits. While the Planning and Zoning Board and City Council worked to reduce the maximum densities permitted in single and multi-family residential zones, the moratorium was extended six times.

Arvida, which owned 1,555 acres in University Park rezoned by the city, filed suit in the circuit courts. Saying the company was only protecting its stockholders, Arvida asked the court to rule both the cap and the rezoning unconstitutional. Three months later Keating-Meredith Properties, Inc., a condominium developer upset by the 40 percent reduction in the maximum density of multi-family zones, also filed suit, as did the Boca Villa Corporation.

At the same time, Arvida campaigned to de-annex University Park from the city. De-annexation needed the approval of the state legislature. While Arvida at first gained the support of the county's legislative delegation, the voters gave the proposal an

overwhelming defeat in an April 1973 election. Although the vote was only a preference poll and not legally binding, the delegation nonetheless reversed its previous stand. In the same election the electorate also turned down a proposed compromise worked out by Councilman William Cruickshank and Arvida officials. Arvida agreed to drop its de-annexation proposal in return for greater densities in University Park. The opposition had called the proposal "blackmail."

In 1976 all Boca Raton city zoning ordinances passed after November 7, 1972, were struck down in Palm Beach County Circuit Court. Judge Thomas Sholts ruled that the city arrived at the forty-thousand cap figure arbitrarily and that it bore no "rational relationship to any permissible municipal objective." Nonetheless, Judge Sholts allowed all local zoning laws to remain intact until all legal appeals were exhausted. Boca Raton decided to fight for the growth cap and appealed to Florida's Fourth District Court of Appeals which upheld Judge Sholts decision. Both the Florida Supreme Court, and in October 1980 the United States Supreme Court, refused to hear Boca Raton's appeal. Eight years after city voters overwhelmingly passed the growth measure, and with over a million dollars in court costs spent by city officials, Boca Raton finally admitted that the growth cap was dead.

Yet by 1980, Boca Raton citizens believed that although they lost every legal battle, they ultimately won the war. In 1979 the city adopted a comprehensive land-use plan mandated by the Florida legislature. This plan placed density ceilings on all properties in the city. City officials could argue that the comprehensive plan achieved in fact what the growth cap failed to accomplish in the courts. While some property owners criticized the cost of the court battle, Mayor William Konrad said "pushing it to the Supreme Court bought time." This was true because Judge Sholts allowed local zoning law to remain intact until the final appeal. As General Richard Mayo, one of the leaders of the cap movement, said, "We achieved what we went after, development can't rebuild what's already on the land." The *Boca Raton News* pointed out that the actual number of housing units in the city were nearly identical under the comprehensive plan as mandated under the growth cap. The growth cap's value as a stalling action could be seen as insuring Boca Raton would never turn into an "asphalt and neon jungle" like Fort Lauderdale or Miami.

While many local residents worked to limit overall growth in the city, as early as 1977, some Boca Raton citizens specifically pointed to what the active development of the western suburbs meant for the downtown area. In particular, the 1979 opening of Town Center shopping mall, in what certainly was far from the center of Boca Raton, brought home to many that the real downtown was in trouble. Although Arvida developed many of the western subdivisions and was a partner in Town Center, it still owned much property in the downtown area. William Shubin, president of Arvida's Industrial-Commercial Division, pointed out the long-range implications for the downtown with Town Center and Interstate-95 reorienting the community's shopping patterns. Shubin said that city fathers had deprived the downtown area of money for "parks, recreation and medians." He and others called for action to revitalize the downtown area.

Urged on by area businessmen, the city ordered a study of the downtown. One planning firm found the intersection of Palmetto Park Road and Federal Highway "one of the best examples of commercial blight in the state." Another claimed "you could pass through the downtown and never know you were there," while a third described the business district as having a "desert-like quality . . . with undistinguished architecture." "Blighted" became the operative word as a Florida law allowed city councils to establish politically independent agencies to reclaim blighted areas. Convinced of the necessity to aid downtown, the Boca Raton City Council created the Community Redevelopment Agency in 1980 with the mandate to return economic vitality to the city's 344-acre central core.

Appointed from Boca Raton's business and civic leaders, the Community Redevelopment Agency Board immediately hired a Philadelphia planning and consulting firm to prepare a plan to revitalize the downtown. The Philadelphia firm, working with a Florida Atlantic University faculty member, forged a comprehensive program that called for bringing new office buildings, improving roads, water, and sewer systems, adding residential units, emphasizing the major historical sites, and unifying the downtown district with new landscaping and street furniture. With the major goals accepted by the agency's board and the City Council, the consultant then urged the agency to complete one demonstration project so that citizens could see concrete results from the plans.

The Boca Raton Historical Society, founded in 1972 as a project of the Junior Service League, grew rapidly, both in membership and the size of its collections, and by 1975 needed a permanent home. In that year the local Bicentennial Committee asked City Council to make the old City Hall available for a museum. The city planned to add to the new City Hall, centralizing the major municipal offices at the Palmetto Park Road location. Since old City Hall, a 1926 Spanish Revival building originally designed by Addison Mizner during the boom period and completed in 1927 by William Alsmeyer, a Delray Beach architect, would then be vacant, the city agreed to its use as a museum and designated it as a historical site. In April 1976 the historical society moved its offices to the second floor of the building, space that had once served as the apartment for the fire chief and his family.

By fall 1982 with work on the additions to new City Hall nearing completion, city officials signed an agreement with the historical society leasing the entire building and authorizing its restoration. The next summer saw the removal of the city offices and the beginnings of restoration work. Jamie Snyder, a historical society board member and former president, also sat on the board of the Community Redevelopment Agency. The agency was still looking for a demonstration project to illustrate its commitment to the downtown. Across Federal Highway from old City Hall stood little Sanborn Square, a 1955 gift to the city from Mrs. Eleanor I. Sanborn in memory of her husband, Dr. William E. Sanborn, a Detroit dentist and winter resident of Boca Raton.

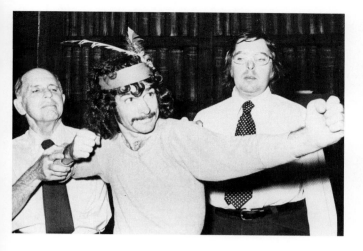

Although the city decorated a tree in the center of the park each Christmas, its stark and sun-drenched boundaries remained vacant throughout most of the year.

Snyder saw revitalization of Sanborn Square as both a compliment to the restored old City Hall and the project that could launch the Community Redevelopment Agency's efforts in the downtown. Soon she received a commitment from banker Charles Schmidt to donate the land north of Boca Raton Road to double the size of the little park. Alexander Suto, an attorney with offices on Boca Raton Road gave $30,000 to purchase forty-foot-tall royal palm trees, other city residents made smaller gifts, and William Cox, the restoration architect for old City Hall, donated a new park plan. The City Council then agreed to close a block of Boca Raton Road to join the old square with Schmidt's gift. Although business and civic leaders hailed the park plan as the needed catalyst for the downtown, a small group of merchants with shops on Boca Raton Road believed the closing of the street would hurt business by cutting direct access from Federal Highway. The owner of the Shady Lady Flower Shop collected enough signatures to force a city-wide vote on the street closing. Both the Community Redevelopment Agency and city council saw the issue in terms of the community's support for downtown revitalization and waged a successful campaign to approve the closing of the street.

The new one-acre park, across from old City Hall, now officially renamed Town Hall after its restoration, attempted through its design and use of materials to demonstrate what Community Redevelopment Agency planners had in mind for the new downtown. An entrance gate, fountain, walkway, and towering royal palm trees aligned with the main entrance to Town Hall across Federal Highway. A second palm-lined axis ran from a large wall fountain at the south end of the

park to an airy arched band pavilion on the north end. The park architecture used postmodern forms to echo the Spanish Revival style of Town Hall. The materials chosen for the walks, terra cotta and green ceramic tiles and cast stone pavers, made to look like key stone, were proposed for use throughout the downtown area as were the street lights and metal park benches. *Miami Herald* architecture critic Beth Dunlap found the new park "intimate and tranquil" and said it could "truly be an old-fashioned village green." Most Boca Raton residents seemed to agree. Soon citizens scheduled small concerts, community events, and even weddings at the new park.

William Miller, director of the S. E. Wimberly Library at Florida Atlantic University, and author Otto L. Bettmann, volunteer rare book librarian and founder of the Bettmann Archives, are pictured before a display of "rarities" from the university collections. Local novelist Theodore Pratt gave all of his manuscripts to Florida Atlantic University. Bettmann, going through another collection of documents donated to the library, found a rare Civil War letter.

Florida Atlantic University

The successful completion of the park failed to act as the hoped for catalyst for downtown redevelopment. The agency knew that people had to be brought into the central core and to do that offices, stores, and jobs had to be created. Help seemed at hand when George Barbar, developer of Woodfield Hunt Club and other residential properties in western Boca Raton, proposed to build three office buildings, a hotel, and a 1,700-car garage on seven square-blocks of vacant downtown land to the west and south of the NCNB Building which he also owned. Barbar, who was born in Lebanon in 1933, made his fortune as an auto dealer in Jamaica before coming to Boca Raton in 1975. Barbar said he could make more money developing in the western suburbs, but he felt he "had the opportunity to make a great contribution to the city with the downtown project."

Although the Barbar Center looked like the answer to the Community Redevelopment Agency's prayers, a number of Boca Raton citizens disagreed. Some objected to the massive scale (the office building planned for Palmetto Park Road and Federal Highway was sixty feet higher than the NCNB Building), others disliked the "glass box" architecture, claiming it was more suited to Houston, home of its architect, than Boca Raton, and some, according to *Florida Trend Magazine*, resented Barbar's "self-promotion." In another "downtown" referendum 60 percent voted against the Barbar project.

Barbar immediately reaffirmed his commitment to the downtown and commissioned Coral Gables architects Spillis, Candela and Partners to redesign the center in a style more compatible to the city's Mediterranean flavor and on a scale more in keeping with the low-rise downtown. Although the new design won city approval, an estimated $50 million was added to the cost of the project, postponing the date for groundbreaking.

Downtown redevelopment seemed to be in a shambles in 1985 when the Community Redevelopment Agency board named Jamie Snyder its new chairman. Her successful masterminding of the rebuilding of Sanborn Square seemed the one bright spot in the agency's otherwise lackluster record. Snyder had come to Boca Raton in the mid-seventies when her husband, Stephen, a former Greyhound executive, purchased the Jai-Alai fronton in Dania. A member of the Junior League, she immediately became involved with numerous volunteer activities in the community. The chairmanship of the Community Redevelopment Agency now became a fulltime unpaid job.

As chairman, one of Snyder's first actions was to recruit Joyce Costomiris to run the agency. The new director had completed a master's thesis at Florida Atlantic University in 1983 on the "Economics of Preservation: Miami Beach and Palm Beach." Her research gave her an understanding of the problems of South Florida. With the postponement of the Barbar Center, Snyder and Costomiris now searched for other projects to bring jobs and people to the downtown. Snyder later said "We were in a disaster situation, . . . People were really distressed and depressed."

In the early months of Snyder's leadership the agency could point to several small projects in the redevelopment area such as the construction of the William Youngerman Building with its small gold dome and Barry Plaza, and the help it gave to the historical society in arranging financing for the purchase of the Florida East Coast Railway depot. In this period William Cox, Jim Mozley, and Grant Thornbrough, planning and landscaping consultants for downtown, also completed their vision for the revitalization of the area which the agency entitled "A Renaissance In the Making." Their proposal, contained in a beautiful brochure with a map and sketches of existing and proposed structures, was inspired by the "pedestrian-oriented layout of Rome." Accordingly, the plan called for the entire area to be unified by landscaping and the materials and street furniture used in remaking Sanborn Square. The planner's map also showed "Central Park," a proposed cultural center, at the location of the Boca Raton Mall.

Many city residents believed the Boca Raton Mall was the most blighted structure in downtown. Quickly constructed in the late sixties with Jefferson's and Britt's department stores as its anchors, by the mid-eighties both were out of business and much of the mall stood vacant. Although it sat on some of the most valuable real estate in the entire city, the mall seemed downscale in upscale Boca Raton, an unattractive monolithic building surrounded by acres of usually vacant parking lots. It soon became evident that Snyder had found her new focal point for downtown redevelopment as Boca Raton residents began hearing of "Art Park." To replace the mall, seen by many as a "white elephant" and a "multi-million-dollar failure," the agency now proposed a cultural center with theatres, concert halls, science and art museums, shops, restaurants, and residences, all in a lush park setting.

While the overall downtown plan met opposition from some property owners, city council approved the proposal which included $50 million for redevelopment with $17 million coming from downtown businesses in special assessments. The agency earmarked this money for the improvement of the road, sewer, and water systems and for the new landscaping and street furniture. The "art park" plan could cost up to $100 million and Snyder realized that she lacked support for a bond issue of that size. Instead, she turned to the private sector to look for a partner. She found that although most local businessmen praised the plan, they had no desire to invest in the downtown.

Among the businessmen Snyder approached was Thomas J. Croker, developer of the Crocker Center and Crocker Plaza office tower in western Boca Raton. He later said, "I viewed (the cultural center) as a pipe dream, but that's because I didn't know Jamie." At first Crocker though it would be "a neat place" to take his children, after someone else built it. Snyder soon convinced him that it could be built and that he should do it. Snyder called for the Community Redevelopment Agency to buy the mall and then hire Crocker to construct the center. With the project now becoming a possibility, the agency decided to seek a formal name. Mizner Park was quickly decided upon.

Construction of the IBM facility in Boca Raton began in 1967 and continued into the 1980s. The monumental interconnected double Y-shaped structures were based on a research center Marcel Breuer and Robert Gatje designed for IBM in LaGaude, France. The Boca Raton complex housed the laboratories and offices where IBM personnel, headed by Philip "Don" Estridge, designed and built the personal computer in just one year's time. The IBM-PC, introduced in August 1981 revolutionized the small computer market and American life.
Courtesy IBM

The agreement between the Community Redevelopment Agency and Crocker called for the agency to purchase the Boca Raton Mall property by issuing thirty-year tax-free redevelopment bonds. Crocker, after razing the old mall, would then build offices, shops, restaurants, movie theatres, and either a hotel or residences on part of the site. The land-rent paid by Crocker would be used to retire the bonds. Should that be insufficient, the Community Redevelopment Agency could also use its tax increment funds generated by new downtown construction and property appreciation. In other words, the agency could claim the project would "literally" pay for itself. The agency also reserved areas within Mizner Park for various cultural organizations who would receive dollar-a-year leases and then construct their own buildings on the thirty-acre site. The Community Redevelopment Agency planned to aid such institutions as the Caldwell Theatre, the Children's Museum, the Science Museum, the Boca Raton Museum of Art, and perhaps even the Philharmonic Orchestra of Florida in fundraising, though they would build and own their own facilities.

Crocker, who said he became as "emotionally attached" to Mizner Park as Snyder, discovered opposition to the project from some Boca Raton Mall merchants and city residents who feared higher taxes. Saying "we want to remove any kind of controversy or taint to the project," Crocker now called for a city-wide referendum on Mizner Park. Before voters went to the polls in late January 1989 the *Boca Raton News* business editor, Patricia Elich, moderated a roundtable discussion between Crocker and Costomiris, and a number of citizens who claimed opposition to Mizner Park. In the discussion Vald Svekis, owner of a mall bookstore, record store, and computer software store, said that while at first he opposed the project, he

planned to reopen in the new center and even add a cappucino bar. Allen Christy, the owner of the mall's one "holdout" bar, said that Crocker had been fair in all his dealings and that "the publicity has helped business." The leader of the citizens' group seemed to have little understanding of the project or of its financing and his statements provided the forum for Crocker and Costomiris to explain the ideas behind the need for involvement by a government agency in the project and the plans for the financing of the park. In concluding the discussion Christy said that he "support(ed) the project, even though it hurts my own business." The voters overwhelmingly agreed, approving Mizner Park by a 7,000 to 4,212 margin.

Crocker had purchased the Boca Raton Mall in March 1988 to facilitate the construction of the park. Shortly after the referendum the Community Redevelopment Agency bought the land from Crocker and then leased him the site for his retail and office complex. Over the summer the old mall came down and architects completed final plans for the new center. The new design, approved by the agency in September 1989, called for a wide landscaped "main street" with large trees and fountains. Stores and offices faced the central plaza on both sides. Jorge Camejo, the new director of the Community Redevelopment Agency, defended the changes in design as both practical and aesthetic improvements.

In June 1989 the Boca Raton Museum of Art chose Moshe Safdie, the Israeli-born Canadian architect to design its new Mizner Park building. Safdie first became widely known as a result of Habitat, a project he designed for Montreal's Expo '67. Since then he had completed several museums including the National Gallery of Art in Ottawa and the Museum of Civilization in Quebec City. Safdie saw the Boca Raton Museum, which was to be the south "anchor" of

Mizner Park, in a "setting where outdoor and indoor spaces relate. Gardens that lead inside the building. Courtyards that are encloseable." Museum director Roger Selby told the *Palm Beach Post* that fundraising had already started and that he hoped to break ground by mid-1991.

As the museum and other organizations inaugurated fundraising campaigns they experienced difficulty finding the millions of dollars needed to build their new facilities. Unfortunately, many leaders in these organizations blamed the Community Redevelopment Agency for their problems. The *Boca Raton News* pointed out that even without the cultural organizations, Mizner Park could be considered a success for the Community Redevelopment Agency. Calling it a "high-quality and enduring attraction for this city," the *News* continued, "It will bring people to the downtown. It will provide additional jobs downtown. And it will help rejuvenate the core of this city." This was what Snyder and the agency set out to accomplish. In July 1990, the board of the Museum of Art, confirmed its decision to move to Mizner Park. The original plans called for the various cultural organizations to build in Mizner Park over a period of

several years, other organizations probably will follow the art museum.

The earliest Arvida developments attempted to define Boca Raton as a special community. As the city's population grew from 922 in 1950 to beyond 60,000 in 1990, Boca Raton attracted people who were at odds with the out-of-control development they saw in other South Florida cities. This new population, a blend of upper income retirees, Florida Atlantic University faculty, IBM engineers, and executives in businesses in surrounding communities who saw Boca Raton as the place to live and raise their families, helped insure that the city retained its special image. These people demanded a sign code so strict that it denied golden arches to McDonald, zoning codes so stringent that no automobile dealership can locate in the city, public beaches that reach almost from city line to city line, and even a limitation on growth itself. As Boca Raton enters the decade of the nineties, it has become the most prestigious city on the Florida Gold Coast. With its caring, concerned, and involved citizens, clean industries, and educational and cultural institutions, Boca Raton's future continues to look bright.

Groundbreaking for additions and remodeling of the new City Hall found representatives from three levels of government manning the shovels. Second from the left is Mayor William Konrad, then Councilman Al Edmunds, Congressman Dan Mica, an unidentified participant, City Attorney Mac Conahan, State Representative Carol Hanson (a former council member), and Councilman Alan Alford.

When the Boca Raton Historical Society received the City Council's promise that the old City Hall could become a museum and the society's headquarters, it immediately began a fundraising campaign. One 1976 project helped celebrate the fiftieth anniversary of the Boca Raton Hotel and Club. "The Mizner Affair," a champagne brunch at the hotel, found society members Margaret Manser, Marylew Redd, Sandra Pearce, Dorn Lee Redd, and Kathy Dickenson setting the mood for the party. The antique automobile was from the collection of Benjamin Caskey.

One of the most successful continuing projects of the historical society is the weekly guided tour of the Boca Raton Hotel and Club. Much of this success is due to Joan Bream, shown seated, who has chaired the tours for almost a decade. With Mrs. Bream at the 1983 society's annual coffee at the hotel were Ruth Statzman and Emilie Heath who served as guides, and in the middle Phyllis Parks, who managed the gift and book store in Town Hall.

In 1980 the historical society gave a Christmas tea on the loggia of the Boca Raton Hotel and Club. Holding antique toys that decorated the base of the tree are society members Doris Ann Stephens, Jamie Snyder, Joan Wargo, and Sara Jane Sylvia.

The Boca Raton Hotel and Club allowed the historical society to conduct tours through the building during the August 1978 Boca Raton Festival Days. The society discovered that thousands of area residents had never seen the inside of the club and would willingly pay for the chance to tour the historic structure. This large group was particularly lucky to have Doris Ann Stephens, a president of the society and wife of L. Bert Stephens, the hotel's president, as its guide. Mrs. Stephens is on the far left.

Although most city offices moved out of the old Municipal Building in 1964 with completion of the new City Hall, the overburdened building department very quickly filled up the space that originally housed all city offices. What had once served as the council chambers became the over-crowded room where Boca Raton citizens applied for building permits.

When the Boca Raton Historical Society moved its offices and archives to the attic-like space on the second floor of the old Municipal Building in April 1976, the city of Boca Raton promised that the entire building would become available as a museum once the additions to the new City Hall were completed. Over the years the city government had made a number of unsympathetic changes to the exterior of the building. These included additions to the south and west of the original structure, enclosing of the fire engine garage, installation of aluminum awning windows, and many coats of white paint that had minimized all the original architectural detailing.

Ribbon-cutting ceremonies in November 1984 officially opened Boca Raton's Town Hall. The city Building Department moved to the new City Hall in the summer of 1983, allowing the historical society to begin restoration of the entire building. The project, with William Cox serving as restoration architect and Diane DeMarco as contractor, restored the structure to the simple elegance of the 1926 original. Although the twenties plans called for a gold dome, the near bankrupt town used silver paint instead. The restored Town Hall came complete with gold dome, topped by a flagpole.

The restoration of Town Hall saw the fire engine bay rebuilt (the space had been used for offices) and the installation of glass doors so that travelers on Federal Highway might see "Old Betsy," the town's original 1926 LaFrance fire engine. The Fire Department loaned Boca Raton's first fire truck to the historical society which made it the centerpiece for the gift and bookshop. The fire engine bay and Old Betsy became the particular attraction of school children visiting Town Hall.

With the removal of the fluorescent lighting and the refinishing of the pecky cypress ceiling and the original hardwood floors, the council chamber once more offered an inviting space for the historical society and many other groups to hold meetings. Although the historical society raised over half-a-million dollars to restore Town Hall, it remained the property of the city of Boca Raton. The restored facilities are accordingly made available for meetings and social events to non-profit groups without charge.

The historical society created its spacious library and archives from two former offices. Bookshelves, protected by glass doors, contain the society's growing book and periocical collections on Boca Raton and South Florida history. Archivist Peggy McCall also uses the glass cases for changing displays of the society's collections which include many items from Mizner Industries such as lamps, iron work, tiles, and pottery. Most of the library furniture, and many other pieces in the building also came from Mizner Industries. Thus the restored building itself has become a living museum of Boca Raton history.

In 1981 the Florida Trust for Historic Preservation met at the Boca Raton Hotel and Club. Marylew Redd, former historical society president and member of the Boca Raton Historic Preservation Board, and Sanford Smith, the board's administrator, discuss preservation issues with Florida's Secretary of State George Firestone. The state's historic preservation division was centered in Secretary Firestone's department.

At the 1981 Florida Trust meeting at the Boca Raton Hotel and Club, Secretary of State George Firestone presented Rhea Chiles the Trust's annual award for preservation for her "keen interest and active participation" in the restoration and use of Florida House. The restored townhouse, across from the United States Capitol in Washington, offered a place for Florida visitors to rest and secure information about the capital city. Senator Lawton Chiles is shown congratulating Mrs. Chiles on the award, held by Secretary Firestone. Kathy Dickenson spoke at the luncheon on the history of Boca Raton.

This late 1960s photograph of downtown Boca Raton shows
the recently completed First Bank and Trust Building (today
NCNB) with its drive-in teller building across the street to the
left. Above and to the right of the drive-in teller building is the
original First Bank and Trust building. After George Barbar
purchased the NCNB Building he announced a large
development on seven downtown blocks that included office
buildings, a garage, and a hotel. A referendum forced Barbar
to scale down his plans and to postpone construction.

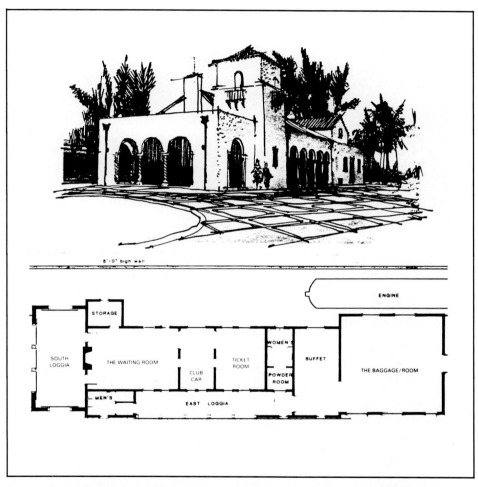

After the Florida East Coast Railway ended passenger service in 1963 the Boca Raton depot quickly became the target of vandals. As the Mediterranean Revival building, constructed in 1930 as the gateway to the Boca Raton Club, deteriorated into an eyesore, the FEC threatened its demolition. As early as 1974 the Boca Raton Historical Society was committed to saving the depot. Shortly after the restoration of Town Hall, the railroad agreed to give the old depot to the historical society, though because it was in receivership, it had to receive a fair market value for the land. The society took title to the depot on January 31, 1985, after the Community Redevelopment Agency helped secure financing from a consortium of ten local banks. To raise the million dollars needed to pay the banks and restore the building, the society launched its second major fundraising campaign under the direction of former president Anne Merrill. William Cox once more agreed to serve as restoration architect.

Jamie Snyder first came to public notice in Boca Raton as president of the historical society. An original appointee to the Board of the Boca Raton Community Redevelopment Agency in 1980, she spearheaded the revitalization of Sanborn Square, making it a demonstration project for the entire redevelopment of downtown. When the agency needed a new chair in 1985, the board named Snyder. Her dynamic leadership resulted in the construction of Mizner Park, Boca Raton's new town center.

The theme of the depot fundraising campaign became "Get On Board." The society also used the railroad motif to set "categories for giving." For $500 one became a conductor, $10,000 brought recognition as a dispatcher, $50,000 signified tycoon status, while very large gifts made the donor a baron. Count Adolph and Countess Henrietta de Hoernle, seen here in 1988 with Kathy Dickenson, chair of the restoration committee, brought the fundraising over the top and added "baron" to their other titles. In recognition of their generosity, the restored depot was officially named the Count Adolph de Hoernle Pavilion.

When William Sonoma, the San Francisco-based kitchenware store opened in Crocker Center in 1986 its party benefited the Boca Raton Historical Society. Sipping California champagne are Helen Popovich, third president of Florida Atlantic University; Barbara and Tom Crocker; and Mary Miller.
Photograph by Louise Yarbrough

The Marriot Hotel at the Crocker Center showed its interest in Boca Raton history by naming some of its meeting rooms for pioneer figures. Shown at the August 18, 1987 dedication of the Captain T. M. Rickards Boardroom are his grandchildren, Marion Rickards Kreale, Thomas M. Rickards III, and Norma Rickards Briggs. The Captain's ledger, 1900 map of Boca Raton which he surveyed, and family photographs are in the collection of the Boca Raton Historical Society.

By 1984 few people ever entered the shabby little Sanborn Square in the heart of Boca Raton's downtown. Under the direction of Jamie Snyder the Community Redevelopment Agency made the square across from Town Hall a demonstration project for the revitalization of downtown. The new royal palm-lined axis centered on the front door of Town Hall.

183

The Pioneer Tea at the Boca Raton Hotel and Club in 1982 found a large group of early Boca Raton residents in attendance. In the front row are J. B. Wiles, Diane Gates Benedetto, Ruby Turner, Theola Edwards Muller, Eula Purdom Raulerson, Pauline Raulerson Aylward, and Margret Olsson. In the middle row are Harold Turner, Max Hutkin, Lucille Zimmerman Morris, and Dixie Hillegas. In the back row are Martha Mahler Holst, Helen Howard, Herbert Brown, F. Byron Parks, David Ashe, Arlene Brittian Owens, and Carl Douglas.

The Boca Raton Historical Society began hosting annual receptions for Boca Raton pioneers in the early 1970s. This December 1980 tea was held in the Boca Raton Hotel and Club. In the front row from the left are Viola Purdom Poston, Lucille Zimmerman Morris, Floy Cooke Mitchell, Eula Purdom Raulerson, Essie Mae Roseke, William Roseke, and Clara Marks. In the top row are Odis Tanner, Helen Howard, Theola Edwards Muller, Martha Maher Holtz, Pauline Raulerson Aylward, David Ashe, and a visitor who lived in the town during WWII.

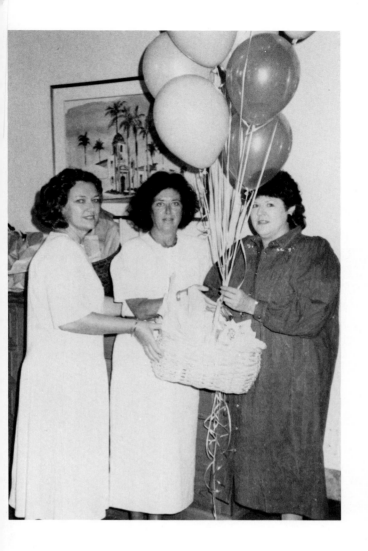

With the maintenance cost of two buildings, the salary of the administrator, as well as the ongoing expenses of collecting historical artifacts and papers, building a library, and publishing the Spanish River Papers, the Boca Raton Historical Society found fundraising had become an almost constant concern. Christine Critchfield, President Kate Toomey, and First Vice President Nancy Schmidt prepare for another appeal for donations for the society in this 1988 photograph.

Dr. Charles Goby, longtime board member, President Nancy Pomar, and Board Chairman Robert Tylander are seen at the member's reception following the annual meeting of the Boca Raton Historical Society in 1983.

This is Cooper Carry and Associates' rendering of Mizner Park's courtyard. The great public space, dividing the buildings containing shops, movie theatres, and restaurants, was based on the proportions of Rome's Piazza Navonna. The courtyard's royal palms, splashing fountains, and shady gazebo provide a restful urban space in the heart of downtown. Community Redevelopment Agency

In the summer of 1990 the City Council created the Old Floresta Historic District, the first in Boca Raton. The residents of Old Floresta appeared before the council in pink T-shirts with architect Addison Mizner's initials. The twenty-nine houses he designed, the historic nature of the 1926 subdivision, and the pride property owners took in the neighborhood convinced the council to act. In celebration the Old Floresta neighbors picnicked at this former small Mizner house which Ronald Miller, AIA, remodeled for Dr. and Mrs. Charles Mohaupt.

BIBLIOGRAPHY

"Africa, U.S.A." *The Spanish River Papers* 11, 2 (Winter 1983).

Akin, Edward N. *Flagler: Rockefeller Partner and Florida Baron.* Kent, Ohio: Kent State University Press, 1988.

Ashton, Jacqueline. *Boca Raton: From Pioneer Days to the Fabulous Twenties.* Boca Raton: Dedication Press, 1979.

Austin, Daniel F., and David M. McJunkin. "The Legends of Boca Ratones." *The Spanish River Papers* 9, 3 (May 1981).

Bramson, Seth H. *Speedway to Sunshine: The Story of the Florida East Coast Railway.* Erin, Ontario: Boston Mills Press, 1984.

Britt, Lora Sinks. *My Gold Coast: South Florida in Earlier Years.* Palatka, Florida: Brittany House, 1984.

Brown, Drollene P. "World War II in Boca Raton: The Home Front." *The Spanish River Papers* 14, 1 (Fall 1985).

Carr, Charles C. *Alcoa: An American Enterprise.* New York: Rinehart and Co., 1952.

Chardon, Roland E. "Northern Biscayne Bay in 1776." *Tequesta* 35 (1975).

Chposky, James, and Ted Leonsis. *Blue Magic: The People, Power and Politics Behind the IBM Personal Computer.* New York: Facts on File Publications, 1988.

Curl, Donald W. *Mizner's Florida: American Resort Architecture.* New York: The Architectural History Foundation, Cambridge: MIT Press, 1984.

———. *Palm Beach County.* Northridge, California: Windsor Publications, 1986.

———. *The Pioneer Cook in Southeast Florida.* Boca Raton: The Boca Raton Historical Society, 1975.

Davis, Karen. *Public Faces—Private Lives: Women in South Florida—1870-1910s.* Miami: Pickering Press, 1990.

Dawson, Robert Charles. "A Study of Florida Atlantic University from July, 1961 to July, 1964: An Identification and Description of Critical Incidents that Have Affected the Development of the Institution." Ed.D. dissertation, Florida State University, 1975.

Ettorre, Tony. *Arvida: A Business Odyssey.* Coral Springs, FL: An ECI Publication, 1990.

Fales, Gregg. "A Master of the Wind." *Fiesta* (May 1981).

Fuller, Walter P. *This Was Florida's Boom.* St. Petersburg: Times Publishing, 1954.

Gates, Harley D. *Reminiscences of A Pioneer.* Boca Raton: privately printed, c. 1950.

Hanna, Alfred Jackson, and Kathryn Abbey Hanna. *Florida's Golden Sands.* Indianapolis: Bobbs-Merrill, 1950.

Holst, Ella Elizabeth. "The Life of a Boca Raton Woman." *The Spanish River Papers* 14, 3 (Spring 1986).

Johnson, Stanley, *Once Upon A Time: The Story of Boca Raton.* Miami: Arvida Corporation, 1979.

Johnston, Alva. *The Legendary Mizners.* New York: Farrar, Straus and Young, 1953.

Knott, James R. *Palm Beach Revisited, I: Historical Vignettes of Palm Beach County.* Privately printed, 1987.

———. *Palm Beach Revisited II: Historical Vignettes of Palm Beach County.* Privately printed, 1988.

Lincoln, Freeman. "The Man Who is Buying Up Florida." *Fortune* (September 1956).

Lure of the Sun: A Story of Palm Beach County. Lake Worth, Florida: First Federal Savings and Loan Association, 1967.

Lynfield, Geoffrey. "Theodore Pratt (1901-1969): A Reassessment." *The Spanish River Papers* 12, 3 (Spring 1984).

———. "Yamato and Morikami: The Story of the Japanese Colony and Some of Its Settlers." *The Spanish River Papers* 13, 3 (Spring 1985).

McIver, Stuart B. *Yesterday's Palm Beach.* Miami: E. A. Seemann Publishing, 1976.

Martin, Sidney Walter. *Florida's Flagler.* Athens: University of Georgia Press, 1949.

Miller, Roger H. *The Inside Story: Florida Atlantic University, Its Beginnings and Early Years.* Boca Raton: Florida Atlantic University, 1990.

Montague, Margaret N. "Theodore Pratt: The Florida Trilogy" (*The Barefoot Mailman, The Flame Tree,* and *The Big Bubble.*) M.A. Thesis, Florida Atlantic University, 1978.

Pierce, Charles W. *Pioneer Life in Southeast Florida.* Edited by Donald W. Curl. Coral Gables: University of Miami Press, 1970.

Pozzetta, George F., and Harry A. Kersey, Jr. "Yamato Colony: A Japanese Presence in South Florida." *Tequesta* 36 (1976).

Pratt, Theodore. *The Story of Boca Raton.* St. Petersburg: Great Outdoors Publishing Co., 1969.

Provenzo, Asterie Baker, and Eugene F. Provenzo, Jr. *Education of the Forgotten Frontier: A Centennial History of the Founding of the Dade County Public Schools.* Miami: Dade County Schools, 1985.

Rouson-Gossett, Vivian Reissland, and C. Spencer Pompey, eds. *Like a Mighty Banyan: Contributions of Black People to the History of Palm Beach County.* Lake Worth, Florida: Palm Beach Junior College, 1982.

Taylor, John. "A Clash of Cultures." *Florida Trend* (September 1987).

Tebeau, Charlton W. *A History of Florida.* Coral Gables: University of Miami Press, 1971.

The Thirtieth Anniversary of the Boca Raton Center for the Arts: 1951-1981. Boca Raton Center for the Arts, 1981.

Waldeck, Jackie Ashton. *Boca Raton: A Romance of the Past.* Boca Raton: The Bicentennial Committee of Boca Raton, 1981.

———. "How Boca Helped Win the War." *Boca Raton Magazine* (March/April 1982).

Wells, Sharon. "Pearl City: An Analysis of the Folk History." *The Spanish River Papers* 15 (1986-87).

Winkler, John K. *The DuPont Dynasty.* New York: Reynal and Hitchcock, 1935.

I N D E X

ABOUT THE AUTHORS

Donald W. Curl is an original member of the Florida Atlantic University faculty and chairman of the Department of History. He teaches courses in American and Florida history as well as art and architectural history. His 1984 study *Mizner's Florida: American Resort Architecture* received the Rembert W. Patrick Memorial Prize as the year's best book on Florida history. Dr. Curl serves as chairman of the Boca Raton Historic Preservation Board and is a director of the Historic Palm Beach County Preservation Board, the Historical Society of Palm Beach County, and the Boca Raton Historical Society, for which he edits *The Spanish River Papers.* He is also a member of the Landmarks Commission of the Town of Palm Beach. After receiving his undergraduate and doctoral degrees from Ohio State University, Dr. Curl taught at Kent State University before coming to Florida Atlantic in 1964.

John P. Johnson is the director of the Historic Palm Beach County Preservation Board, an agency in the Florida Department of State. Since 1985 he has authored the "Partners in Progress" section in *Palm Beach County: An Illustrated History* by Donald W. Curl; the *Delray Beach Historic Sites Survey,* and a *Historic Preservation Plan for Palm Beach County.* His special area of interest is business, engineering, and industrial history with over fifteen mitigation reports in the Historic American Engineering Record collection at the Library of Congress. Mr. Johnson received a bachelor's degree from the University of Massachusetts, Amherst and a master's from Bridgewater State College.